Prayer Assemblies for Primary Schools

Prayer Assemblies for Primary Schools

Maurice Harmon & Elaine Mahon

VERITAS

Published 2012 by
Veritas Publications
7–8 Lower Abbey Street
Dublin 1
Ireland

publications@veritas.ie
www.veritas.ie

ISBN 978 184730 402 5

Text copyright © Maurice Harmon and Elaine Mahon, 2012

10 9 8 7 6 5 4 3 2 1

The material in this publication is protected by copyright law. Except as may be permitted by law, no part of the material may be reproduced (including by storage in a retrieval system) or transmitted in any form or by any means, adapted, rented or lent without the written permission of the copyright owners. Applications for permissions should be addressed to the publisher. The publisher has endeavoured to ascertain and attribute copyright were applicable; should copyright remain unattributed, please contact the publisher, who will correct as necessary in any reprint.

Scripture passages are taken from the Contemporary English Version (CEV) Bible. Copyright © 1995 American Bible Society. All rights reserved.

A catalogue record for this book is available from the British Library.

Cover design by Heather Costello, Veritas
Printed in Ireland by Turners Printing Ltd, Longford

Veritas books are printed on paper made from the wood pulp of managed forests. For every tree felled, at least one tree is planted, thereby renewing natural resources.

Nottinghamshire Education Library Service	
E220133428	
Askews & Holts	Oct-2016
200.71	£14.99

In gratitude to Jim Harmon (1942–1993) and Kay Harmon
for the gifts of Life and Faith

For John O'Malley, who brings Faith to Life

Contents

Introduction 9

Term 1
1. Beginning of the School Year 10
2. St Vincent de Paul 12
3. Guardian Angels 14
4. Mission 16
5. St Francis of Assisi 18
6. The Rosary 20
7. All Saints 22
8. All Souls 24
9. The Immaculate Conception of Mary 28
10. Advent 30
11. Advent Penitential Service (For Senior Classes) 36
12. Christmas (St Nicholas) 40

Term 2
1. World Day of Peace 42
2. Catholic Schools' Week 44
3. St Brigid 46
4. Our Lady of Lourdes/World Day of the Sick 48
5. St Valentine 52
6. Ash Wednesday 54
7. Mother's Day 56
8. Lent, focusing on the work of Trócaire 60
9. St Patrick 64
10. St Joseph 68
11. Lenten Penitential Service (For Senior Classes) 70
12. Holy Week 72

Term 3

1. Easter Season	74
2. Mary	78
3. St Columba (St Columcille)	80
4. The Ascension	82
5. Pentecost	86
6. The Holy Trinity	88
7. The Body and Blood of Christ (Corpus Christi)	90
8. Sacred Heart of Jesus	92
9. End of the School Year	94

Other Resources

1. For Board of Management/Staff Meetings	96
a. Beginning of the School Year	96
b. Advent/Christmas	98
c. End of the School Year	100
2. Remembering our School's Founder	102
3. At a Time of Illness	104
4. On the Death of a Student	106
5. On the Death of a Staff Member	108

Prayer Section	110
Music Section	113
Dates of Feast Days	120

Introduction

During our time as diocesan advisers for Religious Education in primary schools, one of the resources that we were asked for most frequently was a book of prayer assemblies. It was heartening for us that, in spite of a myriad of things pressing on their time, busy principals and Religious Education coordinators were determined to find a space for their school communities to join together in prayer. We offer this book in the hope that it will provide easy-to-use and practical ideas for prayer assemblies in primary schools. We do not intend it to be followed slavishly, but rather encourage the user to amend and adapt the suggestions that we have given to best suit the needs of their individual school communities.

Each prayer assembly is led by one individual, a leader. This leader is often the principal, the school chaplain or a teacher in the school. However, you can also consider asking a parent, a parish representative, a member of the Board of Management or a student from a senior class to lead the prayer assembly. It is also suggested that you vary the leader each week, month or term, so that the children experience different styles of prayer leadership. Each assembly will invite the participation of a number of children, either as readers, or to carry objects to the sacred space. It may therefore be convenient to choose one class group to be responsible for each prayer assembly.

Every service begins with some background information for the leader about the theme of that gathering. It then suggests items that can be included in a sacred space, based on the theme. These items always include a cloth, a candle, a Bible and a cross/crucifix. The colour of the cloth will vary, depending on the season of the liturgical year in which the prayer assembly takes place. For example, a violet cloth will always be suggested for Lent and Advent. Each prayer assembly also includes music suggestions which can be found on the accompanying CD. The lyrics of these songs can be found on pages 113–19.

You will notice that many of the prayers, responses and gestures used in these prayer assemblies are the same as those used during the Mass. We do this in the hope that it will enable those children who are less familiar with the Church's liturgy to become comfortable with it.

In addition to those prayer services based on the feast days and seasons of the liturgical year, we have included additional prayers for use on exceptional occasions such as an illness or death within the school community. Again, these should be adapted as appropriate. We have also included shorter prayers that can be used at Staff or Board of Management meetings during the year. We did so because we believe it is important that Catholic schools are communities where we all pray – not just the children!

The Catechism of the Catholic Church defines prayer as '… the raising of one's mind and heart to God' (CCC, 2559). May this book help all those in your school community to raise their hearts and minds in prayer to God.

Maurice Harmon
Elaine Mahon

Term 1

1. Beginning of the School Year

For the Leader: A prayer assembly or school Mass is an appropriate way to mark the beginning of the new school year. Depending on the size of your school, you could invite parents/guardians and grandparents to join you for this gathering. It is important to recognise especially any new members of the school community, including new pupils and families, new teachers and other staff members and, of course, the new Junior Infant class(es).

> **You will need:**
> - Seven children to read
> - Five children to carry symbols to the sacred space
>
> **Sacred Space:**
> - Green cloth
> - Bible, open at Mark 4:2-9
> - Candle
> - A picture of those who are new to the school community, including the new Junior Infant class(es). Alternatively, you can place their names on the sacred space
> - Other items will be added to the sacred space in the procession at the beginning of the service: a school jumper, some books, a football, seeds and a cross/crucifix

Opening Song: ♪ *Together Again* (Track 31)

Leader: In the name of the Father, and of the Son and of the Holy Spirit.

All: Amen.

Leader: Let us begin with our Morning Prayer:

All: Father in heaven, you love me,
you are with me night and day.
I want to love you always
in all I do and say.
I'll try to please you, Father.
Bless me through the day. Amen.

Leader: We gather together today to ask God's blessing on all of us as we begin this new school year. For some of us, it has been just a few months since we were last together. For others, this is the very first time to gather in prayer with our school. Let us begin our assembly by placing symbols that represent our school community in our sacred space.

Reader 1: *(Pause after each sentence, to allow time for the symbols to be carried to the sacred space)*

We bring a school jumper, representing our togetherness in _____ school.
We bring some books. We are learning together.
We bring a football. We are playing together.
We bring seeds. We are growing together.
We bring a cross. We are praying together.

Leader: Loving God,
Help us to learn together, play together, grow together and pray together this year.
Guide us to follow the example set for us by Jesus, your Son and our teacher.
We ask this through Christ our Lord.

All: Amen.

Leader: Jesus told many stories. One of the stories he told was about a farmer who sowed some seeds. Let us listen to what happened to those seeds.

Reader 2: *A reading from the Holy Gospel according to Mark (4:2-9)*
A farmer went out to scatter seed in a field. While the farmer was scattering the seed, some of it fell along the road and was eaten by birds. Other seeds fell on thin, rocky ground and quickly started growing because the soil wasn't very deep. But when the sun came up, the plants were scorched and dried up, because they did not have enough roots. Some other seeds fell where thornbushes grew up and choked out the plants. So they did not produce any grain. But a few seeds did fall on good ground where the plants

grew and produced thirty or sixty or even a hundred times as much as was scattered.

The Gospel of the Lord.

All: Praise to you, Lord Jesus Christ.

Leader: This story, which seems to be about a farmer sowing seeds, could actually be about us here in _____ school. You see, the teachers are like the farmer. They sow the seeds of knowledge about God and God's love for us. The school is like the sun and the rain which help the seeds to grow and blossom. The children are the soil, in which this knowledge will grow and develop. Let us offer our prayers to God, asking for his help, so that we may all work together this year to let the seeds of knowledge take root in our lives. The response to each prayer is 'Lord, graciously hear us'.

All: Lord, graciously hear us.

Reader 3: We pray for our teachers. May God give them the gifts they need to help us this year. Lord hear us. (*Response*)

Reader 4: We pray for our caretaker, secretary, cleaners, Special Needs assistants, and all who help to make our school a great place to be. May God bless their good work. Lord hear us. (*Response*)

Reader 5: We pray in a special way for our new Junior Infant class(es). May they be happy in our school and always know of God's love for them. Lord hear us. (*Response*)

Reader 6: We pray for students in other classes who are new to our school. May we follow the example of Jesus by making them feel welcome and part of our community. Lord hear us. (*Response*)

Reader 7: We pray for all of the students in our school. May we work together to make this school a happy place to be, guided by the example of Jesus, our friend. Lord hear us. (*Response*)

Leader: Let us pray:

Loving God,
We thank you for bringing us all together at the beginning of another school year.
Send your Spirit upon us to be our helper and guide.
May the seeds of knowledge planted in us grow in faith and love.
We make this prayer through Christ our Lord.

All: Amen.

Leader: In the name of the Father, and of the Son and of the Holy Spirit.

All: Amen.

Closing Song: ♪ *This Is The Day* (Track 30)

Term 1

2. St Vincent de Paul

For the Leader: The Memorial of St Vincent de Paul is celebrated on September 27. St Vincent de Paul was born into a poor family in France in 1581. He was ordained a priest in 1600, at the age of nineteen. St Vincent was deeply committed to caring for the poor and the marginalised in society. He founded the Vincentian Order of priests in 1625 and later the Daughters of Charity. Today, his mission is carried on not only in these two religious orders, but also in the lay movement of The Society of St Vincent de Paul (SVP), which was founded by Frédérick Ozanam in 1833. In this prayer service, the school community is invited to reflect on the person of St Vincent de Paul and the work that the SVP organisation carries out in his name.

> **You will need:**
> - Four children to read
>
> **Sacred Space:**
> - Green cloth
> - Bible, open at Matthew 25:31-41
> - Candle
> - Cross/Crucifix
> - Image of St Vincent de Paul
> - Logo of SVP

Opening Song: ♪ *Circle Of Friends* (Track 9)

Leader: In the name of the Father and of the Son and of the Holy Spirit.

All: Amen.

Leader: Let us begin with our Morning Prayer:

All: Father in heaven, you love me,
you are with me night and day.
I want to love you always
in all I do and say.
I'll try to please you, Father.
Bless me through the day. Amen.

Leader: We gather together today to reflect on the life and work of St Vincent de Paul. Vincent was born in France more than four hundred years ago. He had four brothers and two sisters and they were very poor. One thing that was very important for Vincent was following the example of Jesus by caring for those who were poor or sick. At the age of nineteen he became a priest and began to devote his life to prayer and to caring for those who were in need. Let us listen to a passage from the Gospel, which no doubt influenced the life of St Vincent de Paul.

Reader 1: *A reading from the Holy Gospel according to Matthew (25:31-41)*
When the Son of Man comes in his glory with all of his angels, he will sit on his royal throne. The people of all nations will be brought before him, and he will separate them, as shepherds separate their sheep from their goats. He will place the sheep on his right and the goats on his left. Then the king will say to those on his right,

Reader 2: 'My father has blessed you! Come and receive the kingdom that was prepared for you before the world was created. When I was hungry, you gave me something to eat, and when I was thirsty, you gave me something to drink. When I was a stranger, you welcomed me, and when I was naked, you gave me clothes to wear. When I was sick, you took care of me, and when I was in jail, you visited me.'

Reader 1: Then the ones who pleased the Lord will ask,

Reader 3: 'When did we give you something to eat or drink? When did we welcome you as a stranger or give you clothes to wear or visit you while you were sick or in jail?'

Reader 1: The king will answer,

Reader 2: 'Whenever you did it for any of my people, no matter how unimportant they seemed, you did it for me.'

Reader 1: The Gospel of the Lord.

All: Praise to you, Lord Jesus Christ.

Leader: This Gospel reminds us that when we show our love and care for others, we are in fact showing our love and care for Jesus. This was a message that St Vincent really believed in. One way that his work continues today is through a group called the Society of St Vincent de Paul. People who are part of the Society of St Vincent de Paul visit those who are sick or lonely. They give food to people who need it, and try to make sure that everyone is treated with love and respect. Is this something that we do too? Close your eyes for a moment and think about these questions.

♪ *Play Reflective Music* (Track 22)

Reader 4: 'You gave me something to eat': Have you shared food with others? Have you wasted food? (*Pause*)

'You gave me something to drink': Have you left taps running? Have you wasted water? (*Pause*)

'You welcomed me': How do we welcome people to our school? How do you welcome people to your games? Do you include everyone? (*Pause*)

'You gave me clothes to wear': What do you do with clothes that you do not wear anymore? Can you share them with others? (*Pause*)

'You took care of me': Have you shown care for people who are sick? (*Pause*)

'You visited me'. Have you visited people who are lonely, and have no-one to care for them? (*Pause*)

Leader: When you are ready, you can open your eyes. Together, let us pray that we too may follow the example set for us by St Vincent de Paul.

Loving God,
We thank you for the life of St Vincent de Paul, who lived the message of Jesus to care for the poor and the sick.
Bless the Society of St Vincent de Paul, who carry on his great work.
Help us to be more aware of the needs of others in our home, school and parish communities.
We make this prayer through Christ our Lord.

All: Amen.

Leader: In the name of the Father, and of the Son and of the Holy Spirit.

All: Amen.

Closing Song: ♪ *Whatsoever You Do* (Track 32)

Term 1

3. Guardian Angels

For the Leader: The Memorial of Guardian Angels is celebrated on October 2. Marking this special day in your school is a way of reminding children that angels are real, spiritual beings, created by God as his messengers and our helpers. It will also remind them of the importance of praying to their guardian angel, a practice encouraged during prayer assemblies in the second term.

> **You will need:**
> - Eight children to read
>
> **Sacred Space:**
> - Green cloth
> - Bible
> - Candle
> - Cross/Crucifix
> - Images of angels

Opening Song: ♪ *Christ Be Beside Me* (Track 6)

Leader: In the name of the Father, and of the Son and of the Holy Spirit.

All: Amen.

Leader: Let us begin with our Morning Prayer:

All: Father in heaven, you love me,
you are with me night and day.
I want to love you always
in all I do and say.
I'll try to please you, Father.
Bless me through the day. Amen.

Leader: We gather together today to thank God for our guardian angels. Every one of us has an angel as our helper. We can pray to our guardian angel to mind and protect us. Angels have always brought messages to people from God. Let us listen to some stories about angels from the Bible.

Reader 1: It was an angel who told Mary that she would give birth to Jesus. The angel said that she had been chosen by God from among all the women in the world to be the mother of God's only Son. The angel explained to Mary that she was pregnant by the power of God's Spirit, and that her cousin, Elizabeth, was going to have a baby too. Mary told the angel that she would do as God asked.

Reader 2: When Joseph found out that Mary was going to have a baby, he was very worried and upset. So, God sent an angel to Joseph. While he was asleep, the angel told Joseph not to be afraid to marry Mary. Joseph listened to the angel, and he and Mary were married. Soon after Jesus was born, God sent another angel to Joseph. This time, the angel told him to take Mary and Jesus to Egypt, because they were not safe in Bethlehem. Again, Joseph did as the angel said, and the Holy Family was kept safe.

Reader 3: It was an angel who first announced the birth of Jesus to the world. The angel was sent by God to shepherds who were minding their sheep on a hill close to Bethlehem. The angel delivered God's message about the birth of Jesus to the shepherds by saying, 'I have good news for you, which will make everyone happy. This very day a Saviour was born for you.' Then, many other angels came down from heaven and together they praised God.

Reader 4: When it was time for Jesus to begin the work that God had sent him to do, he prepared himself by going into the wilderness for forty days and forty nights. While he was there, he was tempted to give up on the work that God had sent him to do. But, God sent angels to be with Jesus and to help him. An angel was also sent to Jesus on the night before he died. He was praying in the Garden of Gethsemane and he was very upset because he knew he was going to suffer. The angel came from heaven to help him to do what God wanted.

Reader 5: God also sent angels to tell the Good News about Jesus' rising from the dead to his friends. On Easter Sunday morning, Mary and the women went to the tomb where Jesus was buried but the stone that was in front of the tomb had been rolled away.

The women were confused and upset, but angels appeared and said to them, 'Don't be afraid! I know you are looking for Jesus. He isn't here! God has raised him to life, just as Jesus said he would.' The women ran immediately to tell the rest of the disciples what they had been told.

Leader: So, we can see that angels played a major role in the life of Jesus. They delivered messages from God and they helped Jesus at the time when he needed it most. Our guardian angels can also strengthen us when we need help. Together, let us pray to our guardian angels. The response to each prayer is 'Lord, hear our prayer'.

All: Lord, hear our prayer.

Reader 6: Angels sent by God, watch over our Holy Father, Pope _____, our Bishop _____ and our priest(s) _____. Guide them as they lead our Church. We pray to the Lord. *(Response)*

Reader 7: Angels sent by God, protect those who are sick or sad at this time. Help them to know that God is with them. We pray to the Lord. *(Response)*

Reader 8: Angels sent by God, look after everyone here at _____ school. Keep us all safe from harm, and help us to live as friends of Jesus. We pray to the Lord. *(Response)*

Leader: Let's take a moment to pray in silence to our own guardian angel, asking for whatever it is that we need help with today. *(Pause)*

Now, let's say the prayer to our guardian angel:

All: Angel sent by God to guide me,
be my light and walk beside me;
be my guardian and protect me;
on the paths of life direct me.
Amen.

Leader: In the name of the Father, and of the Son and of the Holy Spirit.

All: Amen.

Closing Song: ♪ *Close To You* (Track 10)

3. Guardian Angels

Term 1

4. Mission

For the Leader: October is Mission awareness month. The Church's Mission is found in Jesus' command to, 'Go to the people of all nations and make them my disciples. Baptise them in the name of the Father, the Son, and the Holy Spirit, and teach them to do everything I have told you' (Mt 28:19-20). The focus of this prayer assembly is on those who have shared in this Mission both at home and overseas. It also gives the school community an opportunity to think about how we can all bring the Good News of God's love to others in our home, school and parish communities.

You will need:
- Four children to read
- Images of Mother Teresa, St Patrick and St Thérèse of Lisieux
- Three children to place these images in the sacred space
- The life story of a local missionary or a person or group who is active in the parish community (optional)

Sacred Space:
- Green cloth
- Bible, open at Matthew 28:19-20
- Candle
- Cross/Crucifix
- Map of the world, or globe

Opening Song: ♪ *Go Tell Everyone* (Track 15)

Leader: In the name of the Father, and of the Son and of the Holy Spirit.

All: Amen.

Leader: Let us begin with our Morning Prayer:

All: Father in heaven, you love me,
you are with me night and day.
I want to love you always
in all I do and say.
I'll try to please you, Father.
Bless me through the day. Amen.

Leader: We gather together today to pray in a particular way for those who leave their homes and countries to share with other people the Good News that Jesus brought for us. We call these people Missionaries. We too can be missionaries, because we can also bring the Good News of God's love to others in our home, school and parish communities. Let us listen to what Jesus asks us to do as missionaries:

Reader 1: *A reading from the Holy Gospel according to Matthew (28:19-20)*
Jesus said, 'Go to the people of all nations and make them my disciples. Baptise them in the name of the Father, the Son, and the Holy Spirit, and teach them to do everything I have told you. I will be with you always, even until the end of the world.'

The Gospel of the Lord

All: Praise to you, Lord Jesus Christ.

Leader: Jesus asks us to tell all people about God, and to bring God's love to others. He promises to be with us as we do this. Let us now listen to the stories of some people who have done as Jesus asked:

Reader 2: Blessed Mother Teresa was born in 1910 in an Eastern European country called Macedonia. At the age of eighteen she came to Ireland and became a nun. Soon after, she travelled to India and lived in the city of Calcutta. While teaching in a school, Mother Teresa began to notice the needs of the sick and the dying and so began to work with these people. In doing so she was answering Jesus' call to feed the hungry and care for the sick and dying. Mother Teresa later founded a community of nuns who work with the poorest people in the world, trying to give them a better life. They are called the Missionaries of Charity.

Leader: In silence we take a moment to ask Blessed Mother Teresa to help us to be kind toward others, and to always see Christ in all people.

♪ *Play Reflective Music (Track 22). If you have an image of Blessed Mother Teresa, invite a child to place it in the sacred space. Then invite the reader to continue:*

Reader 2: Mother Teresa said, 'Not all of us can do great things. But we can do small things with great love.' Let us follow her example.

Reader 3: St Patrick was born in Wales. He came to Ireland as a slave boy and worked here for many years. During this time he prayed to God every day. In a dream, Patrick was told that there was a boat that would take him home to Wales, and that he would be free again. Patrick listened to the voice in the dream, and he managed to escape. However, later in his life, he had another dream. In it he could hear the people of Ireland calling him back to tell them about God. He returned to Ireland and told the people about God.

Leader: In silence we take a moment to ask St Patrick to help us to listen to God, and what he is asking us to do.

♪ *Play Reflective Music (Track 22). If you have an image of St Patrick, invite a child to place it in the sacred space. Then invite the reader to continue:*

Reader 3: St Patrick said, 'Let anyone laugh and tease me if they so wish. I am not keeping silent, nor am I hiding the signs and wonders that were shown to me by the Lord.' Let us follow his example.

Reader 4: St Thérèse was born in France in 1873. She was a very holy young girl and at the age of fifteen she entered the convent and became a nun. In everything she did and everything she said, she acted with great love. When she was still a young woman, St Thérèse became very ill and died. She never travelled far, but she still lived the message of Jesus in the way she lived her life each day.

Leader: In silence we take a moment to ask St Thérèse of Lisiuex to help us to act with love in all that we do.

♪ *Play Reflective Music (Track 22). If you have an image of St Thérèse of Lisiuex, invite a child to place it in the sacred space. Then invite the reader to continue:*

Reader 4: St Thérèse said, 'Miss no single opportunity of making some small sacrifice, here by a smiling look, there by a kindly word; always doing the smallest right and doing it all for love.' Let us follow her example.

You may also like to add a local example, such as a missionary (a priest, religious brother or sister or a lay missionary who is working abroad) or a person or group who is active in the local parish community.

Leader: Let us pray:

Loving God,
We want to respond to Jesus' call to tell all people about your love for them.
May we follow the example of Blessed Mother Teresa, St Patrick, St Thérèse and all those who spread your Word in the world.
We make this prayer through Christ our Lord.

All: Amen.

Leader: In the name of the Father, and of the Son and of the Holy Spirit.

All: Amen.

Closing Song: ♪ *Whatsoever You Do* (Track 32)

Term 1

5. St Francis of Assisi

For the Leader: The Memorial of St Francis of Assisi is celebrated on October 4. In this prayer service, we focus especially on St Francis' awareness of and care for God's creation, and remind the children of their responsibility as 'stewards' or 'caretakers' of God's creation. If your school is a Green School, you will see opportunities to link this in with the prayer assembly.

> **You will need:**
> - Six children to read
>
> **Sacred Space:**
> - Green cloth
> - Bible
> - Candle
> - Cross/Crucifix
> - Image of St Francis
> - Some images of animals or small toy animals
> - Some flowers, leaves or evergreen branches
> - Your school's Green Flag, if your school is a Green School

Opening Song: ♪ *Within God's Creation* (Track 33)

Leader: In the name of the Father, and of the Son and of the Holy Spirit.

All: Amen.

Leader: Let us begin with our Morning Prayer:

All: Father in heaven, you love me,
you are with me night and day.
I want to love you always
in all I do and say.
I'll try to please you, Father.
Bless me through the day. Amen.

Leader: We gather today to celebrate the life of St Francis of Assisi. St Francis was like Jesus in the way he loved others and the world around him. Let us listen to the story of his life:

Reader 1: St Francis was born in a place called Assisi, in Italy, over eight hundred years ago. His family had a lot of money, and St Francis could have had anything he wanted when he was growing up. He spent a lot of money on fancy clothes and parties. When St Francis was still a young man, a war broke out in Assisi, and he was taken prisoner. While he was in prison, he had a lot of time to think. St Francis realised that he was living his life in a selfish way. He began to understand that he was not living in the way that Jesus did, and he decided to make a change.

Reader 2: St Francis began to give away his money and his fine clothes. He went to work with people who had leprosy, an awful skin disease. No-one wanted to be near these people, but that didn't stop St Francis. He was soon joined by others, and they worked together to help the people who most needed it. St Francis spent a lot of time outside, and enjoyed caring for animals. He knew that animals were God's creatures too, and that they deserved respect and needed to be cared for. It is said that he spoke to the birds, and that he calmed a dangerous wolf that was scaring the people in a town close to Assisi. We can learn a lot from St Francis of Assisi, including the need to care for those who do not have as much as we do, and the need to care for God's creation.

Leader: Here at _____ school, we follow in the footsteps of St Francis by caring for and valuing the beautiful world that God has given to us. We do this by putting our litter in the bin, by respecting the plants and animals that live and grow around us, and by not wasting precious things like water and energy. Many of us also have pets and animals at home that we care for. Let us ask St Francis to help us to continue our good work of caring for God's creation. We know that when we show our love for the world, we show our love for God. The response to each prayer is, 'St Francis, pray for us.'

All: St Francis, pray for us.

Reader 3: That we may always care for plants and flowers, and never carelessly destroy them. *(Response)*

Reader 4: That we may always treat animals with the care that they deserve, and that we may never mistreat them, or be cruel to them. *(Response)*

Reader 5: That we may always treat people with respect, especially those people who are forgotten about or left out because they are sick or poor. *(Response)*

Reader 6: That we may not be greedy for clothes, toys or other things that we may want, and that we may be happy with what we have. *(Response)*

Leader: Let us pray:

Loving God,
We thank you for the example of St Francis of Assisi.
We ask you to watch over all our pets and animals, and keep them safe.
Help us to live like St Francis of Assisi, by always putting others before ourselves, and by taking care of your wonderful creation.
We make this prayer through Christ our Lord.

All: Amen.

Leader: In the name of the Father, and of the Son and of the Holy Spirit.

All: Amen.

Closing Song: ♪ *All The Nations Of The Earth* (Track 2)

5. St Francis of Assisi

Term 1

6. The Rosary

For the Leader: During the month of October we are invited to give some time to pray the Rosary. The Rosary is a very old prayer in the Catholic Church, and in it we reflect on different events in the life of Jesus. Praying the Rosary is like looking at an album of pictures in the life of Jesus. There are twenty different events that we reflect on and these are called 'Mysteries'. These mysteries are broken into four groups: the Joyful Mysteries, the Sorrowful Mysteries, the Glorious Mysteries and the Mysteries of Light. As part of this prayer service, we will focus on one of the Mysteries of Light: The Baptism of Jesus.

> **You will need:**
> - Five children to read
> - One child to lead a decade of the Rosary
>
> **Sacred Space:**
> - Green cloth
> - Bible, open at Matthew 3:13-17
> - Candle
> - Cross/Crucifix
> - Statue or image of Mary
> - Rosary beads

Opening Song: ♪ *Mary Our Mother* (Track 20)

Leader: In the name of the Father, and of the Son and of the Holy Spirit.

All: Amen.

Leader: Let us begin with our Morning Prayer:

All: Father in heaven, you love me,
you are with me night and day.
I want to love you always
in all I do and say.
I'll try to please you, Father.
Bless me through the day. Amen.

Leader: We gather together today to reflect on the Rosary. Praying the Rosary is like looking at a photo album of the life of Jesus. There are twenty different moments that we reflect on and we call these moments 'Mysteries'. Let us learn some more about these mysteries:

Reader 1: The Joyful Mysteries help us to remember the happy days in the life of Jesus and his mother, Mary. These are: When Mary found out that she was pregnant; when she visited her cousin Elizabeth; when Jesus was born; when Jesus was brought to the Temple to be blessed; and when Jesus was found in the Temple after he had been lost. The names of the Joyful Mysteries are: The Annunciation, The Visitation, The Birth of Jesus, The Presentation and The Finding in the Temple. What great days they were!

Reader 2: The Sorrowful Mysteries remind us of the sad moments in Jesus' life, just before he died. These are: when Jesus was arrested; when the soldiers hurt him; when they placed a crown of thorns on his head; when Jesus was given his cross to carry; and when Jesus died on the cross. The names of the Sorrowful Mysteries are: The Agony in the Garden, The Scourging at the Pillar, The Crowning with Thorns, The Carrying of the Cross and The Crucifixion. Mary was with Jesus during these sorrowful moments.

Reader 3: The Glorious Mysteries begin with the Resurrection, when God raised Jesus to new life. Then comes the moment when Jesus was taken back into heaven, and the day on which the Holy Spirit was given to Jesus' apostles. Finally we remember the day Mary was assumed into heaven, and how she was made Queen of Heaven. The names of the Glorious Mysteries are: The Resurrection, The Ascension, The Descent of the Holy Spirit, The Assumption and The Crowning of our Lady as Queen of Heaven. All of these moments in the lives of Jesus and Mary give glory to God.

Reader 4: The Mysteries of Light help us to recall the public life of Jesus. They begin with his baptism by John, and include his first miracle, when he turned water into wine. We then remember how Jesus told people about God's Kingdom, and how God showed that Jesus was his Son during the Transfiguration. Finally, we remember that Jesus gave us the gift of himself during the Last Supper. The names of the Mysteries of Light are: The Baptism of Jesus in the Jordan, The Wedding at Cana, Jesus proclaims the coming of the Kingdom of God, The Transfiguration and Jesus gives us the Eucharist. All of these moments shed light on who Jesus is.

Leader: Today, let us focus on one of the Mysteries of Light: The Baptism of Jesus. Let us listen to the Gospel story of what happened on that day. Try to picture what happened as you listen. Remember, it is like you are looking through a photo album of Jesus' life.

Reader 5: *A reading from the Holy Gospel according to Matthew (3:13-17)*
Jesus left Galilee and went to the Jordan River to be baptised by John. But John kept objecting and said, 'I ought to be baptised by you. Why have you come to me?'

Jesus answered, 'For now this is how it should be, because we must do all that God wants us to do.' Then John agreed. So Jesus was baptised. And as soon as he came out of the water, the sky opened, and he saw the Spirit of God coming down on him like a dove. Then a voice from heaven said, 'This is my own dear Son, and I am pleased with him.'

The Gospel of the Lord.

All: Praise to you, Lord Jesus Christ.

Leader: When we pray the first Mystery of Light, The Baptism of Jesus, we think about how Jesus went to be baptised by John in the River Jordon. We think about how a dove came from heaven, and about how God's voice announced that Jesus was his Son.

As we think about these things, we pray one Our Father and ten Hail Marys. We finish with one Glory be to the Father. We pray these prayers together, with one person saying one half and the group responding with the other half. Together, then, let's pray this decade of the Rosary, remembering Jesus' Baptism. We can also think about the day on which we were baptised, when we became part of the God's family.

Invite one child to lead the decade of the Rosary. Encourage him/her to use Rosary beads. You can explain to the children that the Rosary beads will help him/her to say the correct number of prayers.

Leader: Let us pray:

Jesus, our friend,
We thank you for the gift of the Rosary, which helps us to reflect on your life, and on the life of your mother, Mary. Help us to pray the Rosary in our home, school and parish communities as a sign that we want to learn more about you, and grow to be like you.
We ask this prayer through Christ our Lord.

All: Amen.

Leader: In the name of the Father, and of the Son and of the Holy Spirit.

All: Amen.

Closing Song: ♪ *Magnificat* (Track 19)

6. The Rosary

Term 1

7. All Saints

For the Leader: The Solemnity of All Saints, more commonly known as 'All Saints' Day' is celebrated on November 1. The saints can be described as ordinary men and women who lived extraordinary lives. Each saint can teach us something about living as a faithful Christian, and so we try to follow their example. Strictly speaking, we do not pray to the saints. Rather, we ask the saints to pray for us, to pray with us, and to bring our prayers to God. The Solemnity of All Saints is a holy day of obligation, so all Catholics should participate in Mass.

> **You will need:**
> - Six children to read
> - The life story of your school/parish/diocese's patron saint (optional)
>
> **Sacred Space:**
> - Red cloth
> - Bible
> - Candle
> - Cross/Crucifix
> - Some pictures or statues of the saints, in particular the patron saint of your school or parish

Opening Song: ♪ *Litany Of The Saints* (Track 18)

Leader: In the name of the Father, and of the Son and of the Holy Spirit.

All: Amen.

Leader: Let us begin with our Morning Prayer:

All: Father in heaven, you love me,
you are with me night and day.
I want to love you always
in all I do and say.
I'll try to please you, Father.
Bless me through the day. Amen.

Leader: We gather together today to remember the saints. Saints are holy men and women who lived good lives, dedicated to God and to others. Let us remind ourselves about some of the saints that we have learned about here in _____ school, and think about what we can learn from them.

You may like to reflect on your school/parish/diocese's patron saint, or a local saint, in place of one of those named below.

Reader 1: The first among all the saints is Mary, Mother of God. She lived a perfect and holy life. She said 'Yes' to God's call to be the Mother of Jesus, even though she was nervous and afraid. Mary teaches us to trust in God.

Reader 2: St Patrick brought the Good News about God's love to the people of Ireland. He taught them about Jesus, and used the shamrock to help them to understand the relationship between God the Father, Jesus and the Holy Spirit. St Patrick teaches us to share the Good News about God with other people.

Reader 3: St Brigid was a kind and generous woman. She helped people who were poor and sick. She also built a church and convent in County Kildare. St Brigid teaches us to look out for and help people who do not have as much as we do.

Reader 4: St Vincent de Paul was a great friend and helper to people who were poor, in prison, or homeless. He gave them whatever they needed and never asked for anything in return. St Vincent de Paul teaches us to share what we have with those who need it.

Reader 5: St Thérèse of Lisieux died when she was just twenty-four years old. However, even in her short life, she managed to bring joy and happiness to the world by doing small acts of kindness for the people she met. St Thérèse teaches us that it is important to do little things with great love.

Reader 6: St Francis of Assisi cared greatly for God's creation. He knew that we need to respect the natural world and to take care of it. We show that we are learning from St Francis when we pick up litter, save energy and water, and are kind to animals.

Leader: We thank God for these holy men and women, and ask them to pray for us, so that we can learn by their example, and live our lives for God and for others. The response to each prayer is, 'Pray for us'.

All: Pray for us.

If you have discussed the life of a saint particular to your school, parish or diocese above, include him/her in place of one of the saints named in the litany below.

Reader 1: Holy Mary, Mother of God. *(Response)*

Reader 2: St Brigid. *(Response)*

Reader 3: St Patrick. *(Response)*

Reader 4: St Vincent de Paul. *(Response)*

Reader 5: St Francis of Assisi. *(Response)*

Reader 6: St Thérèse of Lisieux. *(Response)*

Leader: Let us pray:

Loving God,
The lives of the saints show us how ordinary men and women can live their lives in love for you and for others.
Help us to follow their example.
We make this prayer through Christ our Lord.

All: Amen.

Leader: In the name of the Father, and of the Son and of the Holy Spirit.

All: Amen.

Closing Song: ♪ *Go Tell Everyone* (Track 15)

7. All Saints

Term 1

8. All Souls

For the Leader: The Commemoration of All the Faithful Departed, more commonly known as 'All Souls' Day' is celebrated on November 2. The Church has a great tradition of honouring and respecting the memory of the faithful departed. In this prayer assembly the school community is invited to remember family and friends who have died. You can use it at any time during the month of November.

> **You will need:**
> - Remembrance Tree: Either a bare branch secured in sand in a vase, pot or bowl, or the outline of a tree or branch drawn on a banner, noticeboard or large piece of card/paper
> - One prayer leaf for each person. The template for this leaf is on page 27. These should be completed before the prayer assembly begins, and placed on the Remembrance Tree. One child from each class can keep their prayer leaf as they will add it to the tree during the service
> - A hole-puncher and some string to attach the prayer leaves to the tree
> - Seven children to read
> - One child from each class to place their prayer leaf on the Remembrance Tree
>
> **Sacred Space:**
> - Violet cloth
> - Bible, open at 1 Thessalonians 4:13-18
> - Candle
> - Cross/Crucifix

Opening Song: ♪ *Remember Them* (Track 23)

Leader: In the name of the Father, and of the Son and of the Holy Spirit.

All: Amen.

Leader: Let us begin with our Morning Prayer:

All: Father in heaven, you love me,
you are with me night and day.
I want to love you always
in all I do and say.
I'll try to please you, Father.
Bless me through the day. Amen.

Leader: We gather together today to remember all those we knew and loved who have died. Earlier, we took time to write their names on prayer leaves, and these now hang on our Remembrance Tree. We invite one person from each class to place their leaves on the tree, representing all of our prayers for those who have died.

You may like these children to come forward all together, or to call them one-by-one. You might also like to play Reflective Music (Track 22) as they do so.

Leader: While it may be sad for us to think about people who have died, we know that Jesus brought us Good News. Let us listen to that Good News now:

Reader 1: *A reading from the letter of St Paul to the Thessalonians* (4:13-18)*
We believe that Jesus died and rose again, and that it will be the same for all those who love Jesus. When they die, God will bring them with him. When we die we will meet the Lord in heaven, and stay with him forever.

The Word of the Lord.

All: Thanks be to God.

Leader: Together, let us pray for those who have died. The response to each prayer is, 'May the light of Christ shine on them'.

All: May the light of Christ shine on them.

---
* An adaptation as found in *Alive-O 6*, p. 359.

Reader 2: For all grandparents who have died. *(Response)*

Reader 3: For all parents who have died. *(Response)*

Reader 4: For all past teachers in this school who have died. *(Response)*

Reader 5: For all past priests of our parish who have died. *(Response)*

Reader 6: For those who have died and have no one to remember them. *(Response)*

Reader 7: For all those whose names are included on our Remembrance Tree. *(Response)*

Leader: We know that Jesus prayed constantly to his Father in heaven. He asked us to pray to God the Father too. And so, as Jesus asked us, we dare to say:

All: Our Father …/Ár nAthair …

Leader: Let us pray:

Loving God,
We thank you for the lives of our loved ones who have died.
We ask you to care for those who are missing them at this time.
May we always remember your promise that, one day, we will all be together in heaven.
We make this prayer through Christ our Lord.

All: Amen.

Leader: In the name of the Father, and of the Son and of the Holy Spirit.

All: Amen.

Closing Song: ♪ *Close To You* (Track 10)

8. All Souls

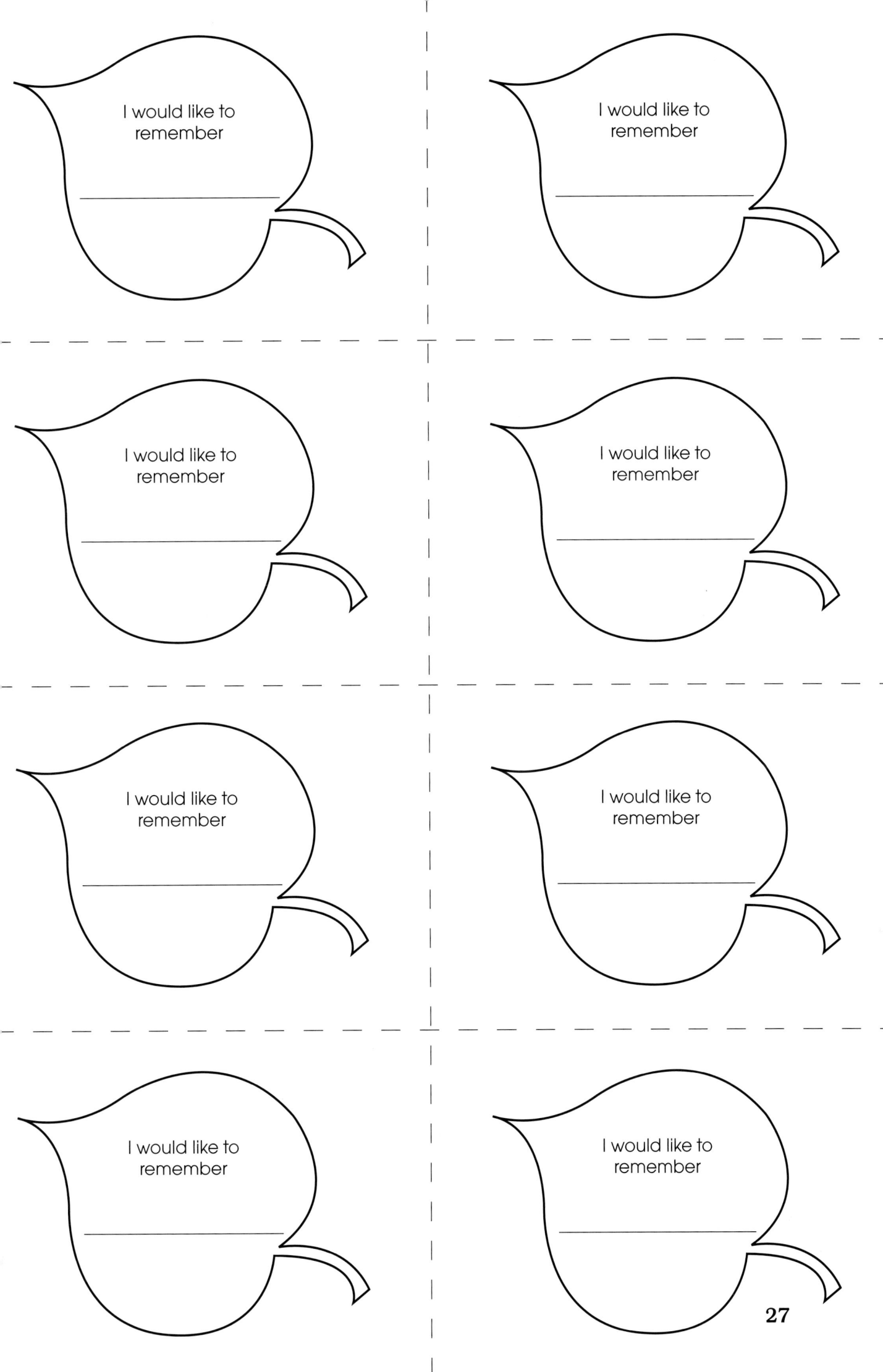

Term 1

9. The Immaculate Conception of Mary

For the Leader: The Solemnity of the Immaculate Conception of the Blessed Virgin Mary is celebrated on December 8. Many people believe that the feast celebrates Jesus' conception, but in fact it celebrates Mary's Immaculate Conception; the fact that Mary was, from the very first moment of her existence (her conception), without sin. That is the focus of this prayer service. We look to Mary as a role model in terms of how to live a life of faith. As today's feast is a holy day of obligation, all Catholics should attend Mass.

> **You will need:**
> - Ten children to read
>
> **Sacred Space:**
> - White or blue cloth
> - Bible, open at Luke 1:26-38
> - An advent wreath, see page 39
> - Cross/Crucifix
> - Statue or image of Mary
> - Rosary beads
> - Flowers

Opening Song: ♪ *Mary, Our Mother* (Track 20)

Leader: In the name of the Father, and of the Son and of the Holy Spirit.

All: Amen.

Leader: Let us begin with our Morning Prayer:

All: Father in heaven, you love me,
you are with me night and day.
I want to love you always
in all I do and say.
I'll try to please you, Father.
Bless me through the day. Amen.

Leader: We gather together today to celebrate a very special feast day – the Immaculate Conception of Mary. The words 'Immaculate Conception' tell us that from the very moment that Mary was born – and even when she was still growing in her mother's tummy – she was free from sin. Imagine that! Mary never hurt or upset anyone. She was never mean or dishonest. She always lived in the way God wanted. Mary was perfect, because God chose her to be the mother of his only Son, Jesus. That is why we say that she is 'full of grace' and 'blessed among woman'. Let us listen to the story of how Mary found out that she had been chosen by God for this special job:

Reader 1: *A reading from the Holy Gospel according to Luke (1:26-38)*
One month later God sent the angel Gabriel to the town of Nazareth in Galilee with a message for a virgin named Mary. She was engaged to Joseph from the family of King David. The angel greeted Mary and said,

Reader 2: 'You are truly blessed! The Lord is with you.'

Reader 1: Mary was confused by the angel's words and wondered what they meant. Then the angel told Mary,

Reader 2: 'Don't be afraid! God is pleased with you, and you will have a son. His name will be Jesus. He will be great and will be called the Son of God Most High. The Lord God will make him king, as his ancestor David was. He will rule the people of Israel forever, and his kingdom will never end.'

Reader 1: Mary asked the angel,

Reader 3: 'How can this happen? I am not married!'

Reader 1: The angel answered,

Reader 2: 'The Holy Spirit will come down to you, and God's power will come over you. So your child will be called the holy Son of God. Your relative Elizabeth is also going to have a son, even though she is old. No one thought she could ever have a baby, but in three months she will have a son. Nothing is impossible for God!'

Reader 1: Mary said,

Reader 3: 'I am the Lord's servant! Let it happen as you have said.'

Reader 1: And the angel left her.

The Gospel of the Lord.

All: Praise to you, Lord Jesus Christ.

Leader: What words would you use to describe Mary? What kind of things can we say about her? *(Invite children to think in silence or to answer aloud, whichever is most appropriate.)*

Mary did what God wanted her to do, so she was faithful or obedient. She was loving and caring, because she looked after the baby Jesus and helped him to grow. Mary was also certainly 'holy'. Let's think about times when you acted like Mary.

♪ *Play Reflective Music* (Track 22).

Close your eyes for a moment. Think of a time when you said 'Yes' when you were asked to do something. Maybe you did some chores at home, or maybe you did what your teacher asked. At those times when you were faithful and obedient, you were acting like Mary. *(Pause)*

Now imagine a time when you showed love to your family or friends. Think about one time when you did a nice thing, like sharing something or giving someone a hug. At those times when you were loving and caring, you were acting like Mary. *(Pause)*

Lastly, think about a time when you stood by someone who needed help. Maybe someone was being picked on in the yard, and you stood up for them. Maybe someone was left out, and you included them. Mary was with Jesus to the very end of his life. At those times when you stood by others, you were acting like Mary. *(Pause)*

When you are ready, you can open your eyes. Together, let us give thanks to God for Mary, the Mother of Jesus. The response to each prayer is 'Thank you, God, for Mary.'

All: Thank you, God, for Mary.

Reader 4: Mary said 'Yes' to God, to be the Mother of Jesus. *(Response)*

Reader 5: Mary and Joseph travelled to Bethlehem, where Jesus was born. *(Response)*

Reader 6: Mary and Joseph cared for Jesus. *(Response)*

Reader 7: Mary and Joseph brought Jesus to the temple to be blessed. *(Response)*

Reader 8: Mary and Joseph found Jesus in the temple when he was lost. *(Response)*

Reader 9: Mary and Jesus went to the wedding at Cana. *(Response)*

Reader 10: Mary was with Jesus when he died on the cross. *(Response)*

Leader: Together, we pray:

All: Hail Mary …/'Sé do bheatha, a Mhuire …

Leader: Let us pray:

Loving God,
We thank you for the example of Mary,
whom you chose to be the mother of your only Son, Jesus.
She lived her life with love for you and for others.
Help us to do the same.
We make this prayer through Christ our Lord.

All: Amen.

Leader: In the name of the Father, and of the Son and of the Holy Spirit.

All: Amen.

Closing Song: ♪ *Magnificat* (Track 19)

9. The Immaculate Conception of Mary

Term 1

10. Advent

For the Leader: Advent marks the beginning of a new Church year. The word 'Advent' means 'coming' or 'arrival'. The season of Advent has two foci: the celebration of the birth of Jesus in his first coming, and the anticipation of his return as Christ the King at the end of time. In this prayer service your school community is invited to reflect on the phrase 'Waiting in joyful hope'. The people who waited for Jesus' arrival on that first Christmas waited in joyful hope. We now remember that and await his second coming, with that same joyful hope.

> **You will need:**
> - Four children to read
> - Three posters, featuring the words 'Waiting', 'Joyful' and 'Hope', which you will find on pages 33–35. You may like to ask children to colour these in before the service begins.
> - Three children to carry the posters to the sacred space
>
> **Sacred Space:**
> - Violet cloth
> - Bible, open at Psalm 130
> - An Advent Wreath, with the correct number of candles lighting, depending on the week in which the prayer service is being celebrated
> - Cross/Crucifix

Opening Song: ♪ *Advent Hymn* (Track 1)

Leader: In the name of the Father, and of the Son and of the Holy Spirit.

All: Amen.

Leader: Let us begin with our Morning Prayer:

All: Father in heaven, you love me,
you are with me night and day.
I want to love you always
in all I do and say.
I'll try to please you, Father.
Bless me through the day. Amen.

Leader: We gather together today to celebrate the season of Advent. It is the season when we wait and prepare for the coming of Jesus. Let us listen to a reading from the Bible which describes how we might feel as we wait.

Reader 1: *A reading from the Book of Psalms (130)*
With all my heart, I am waiting, Lord, for you! I trust your promises. I wait for you more eagerly than a soldier on guard duty waits for the dawn.

The Word of the Lord.

All: Thanks be to God.

Reader 2: Advent is a season of waiting; waiting in joyful hope for the coming of Jesus. We all have to wait in our lives for different things. We wait for friends to come to play. We wait for parents to collect us and we wait for lunch break each day. To wait is part of all our lives. Mary and Joseph waited for the birth of Jesus on that first Christmas. We now wait too.

Child holds up the poster of the word 'Waiting', and places it in the sacred space

Reader 3: Advent is a time of joy. As Mary and Joseph waited during the first Advent, they waited with joy in their hearts for the coming of the baby Jesus. The baby in Elizabeth's womb jumped for joy when Mary went to visit her. We remember and celebrate the joy that the people felt as they waited for the birth of Jesus. We remember these great events as we wait in joy to celebrate the birth of Jesus once again.

Child holds up the poster of the word 'Joyful', and places it in the sacred space

Reader 4: Advent is a time of hope. As Mary and Joseph waited they were filled with hope. The people of Israel waited in hope for the coming of Jesus the Saviour. We look forward to and wait, in joyful hope, to celebrate that first Christmas. We also wait in joyful hope for when Jesus will come again at the end of time.

Child holds up the poster of the word 'Hope', and places it in the sacred space

Leader: Let us pray these words together: We wait in joyful hope.

All: We wait in joyful hope.

Leader: Let us pray:

Loving God,
We thank you for the gift of your Son, Jesus.
As we wait for the celebration of his birth on Christmas day, may we see more clearly the way that leads to him, and wait in joyful hope for his return at the end of time.
We make this prayer through Christ our Lord.

All: Amen.

Leader: In the name of the Father, and of the Son and of the Holy Spirit.

All: Amen.

Closing Song: ♪ *Come And Be Born In Our Hearts* (Track 11)

Waiting

Joyful

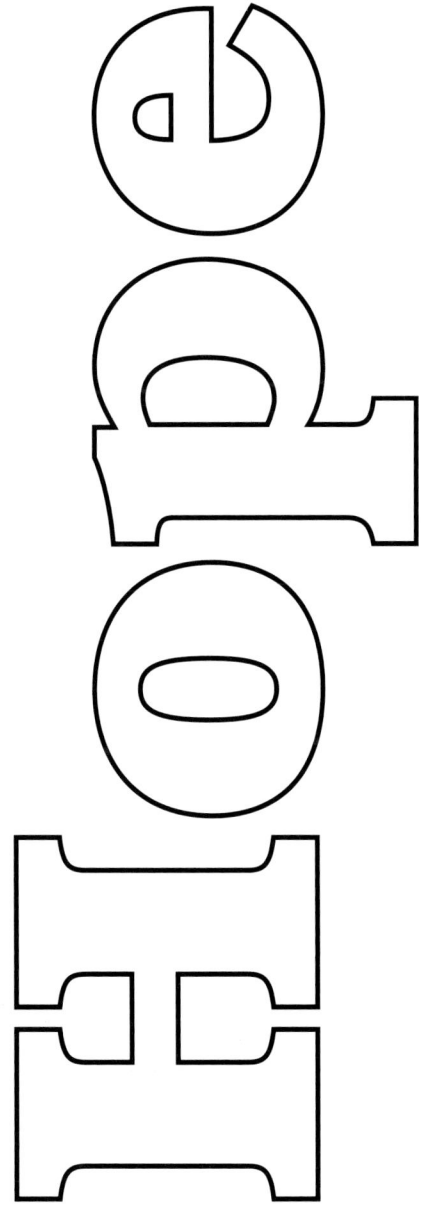

Term 1

11. Advent Penitential Service (For Senior Classes)

For the Leader: Advent is a time of preparation for the joyful season of Christmas. As part of that preparation, we are encouraged to celebrate the Sacrament of Reconciliation as a reminder of God's mercy, love and forgiveness. It may be possible to invite a priest to celebrate the sacrament with the children during this Advent Penitential Service. This could be organised on a class-by-class basis. In this case, the prayer assembly would serve as a preparation for the sacrament, which would be celebrated individually at a later time that day or week. If it is not possible for a priest to be present, use this prayer assembly as a time for those gathered to reflect on the things for which they are sorry, and encourage them to celebrate the Sacrament of Reconciliation in their own time. You might let them know the days and times when the sacrament is celebrated in the parish Church.

> **You will need:**
> - Five children to read
>
> **Sacred Space:**
> - Violet cloth
> - Bible, open at Luke 15:11-32
> - An Advent Wreath, with the correct number of candles lighting, depending on the week in which the prayer service is being celebrated
> - Cross/Crucifix

Opening Song: ♪ *Song Of Repentance* (Track 24)

Leader: In the name of the Father, and of the Son and of the Holy Spirit.

All: Amen.

Leader: Let us begin with our Morning Prayer:

All: Father in heaven, you love me,
you are with me night and day.
I want to love you always
in all I do and say.
I'll try to please you, Father.
Bless me through the day. Amen.

Leader: We gather together today to continue our Advent preparations by reflecting on the times when we did not live in the way Jesus asked. It is important that we do this before we celebrate Christmas, because if we want to celebrate the birth of Jesus in the best possible way, we need to make sure that we are at peace with God and with each other. So, let us take some time to think about the things for which we are sorry.

Leader: For the times when we used words carelessly, and hurt each other, Lord, have mercy.

All: Lord, have mercy.

Leader: For the times when we disobeyed our parents, teachers and those who were trying to help us,
Christ, have mercy.

All: Christ, have mercy.

Leader: For the times when we missed the opportunity to bring your love to others,
Lord, have mercy.

All: Lord, have mercy.

Leader: May almighty God have mercy on us, forgive us our sins, and bring us to everlasting life.

All: Amen.

Leader: We know that God is always ready to forgive us. God loves us no matter what. Jesus told many stories to his friends to teach them about God's never-ending love. One of these stories is about a father and his two sons. Let us listen to the story now.

Reader 1: *A reading from the Holy Gospel according to Luke* (15:11-32)
Once a man had two sons. The younger son said to his father,

Reader 2: 'Give me my share of the property.'

Reader 1: So the father divided his property between his two sons. Not long after that, the younger son packed up everything he owned and left for a foreign country, where he wasted all his money in wild living. He had spent everything, when a bad famine spread through that whole land. Soon he had nothing to eat. He went to work for a man in that country, and the man sent him out to take care of his pigs. He would have been glad to eat what the pigs were eating, but no one gave him a thing. Finally, he came to his senses and said,

Reader 2: 'My father's workers have plenty to eat, and here I am, starving to death! I will go to my father and say to him, "Father, I have sinned against God in heaven and against you. I am no longer good enough to be called your son. Treat me like one of your workers."'

Reader 1: The younger son got up and started back to his father. But when he was still a long way off, his father saw him and felt sorry for him. He ran to his son and hugged and kissed him. The son said,

Reader 2: 'Father, I have sinned against God in heaven and against you. I am no longer good enough to be called your son.'

Reader 1: But his father said to the servants,

Reader 3: 'Hurry and bring the best clothes and put them on him. Give him a ring for his finger and sandals for his feet. Get the best calf and prepare it, so we can eat and celebrate. This son of mine was dead, but has now come back to life. He was lost and has now been found.'

Reader 1: And they began to celebrate. The older son had been out in the field. But when he came near the house, he heard the music and dancing. So he called one of the servants over and asked,

Reader 4: 'What's going on here?'

Reader 1: The servant answered,

Reader 5: 'Your brother has come home safe and sound, and your father ordered us to kill the best calf.'

Reader 1: The older brother got so angry that he would not even go into the house. His father came out and begged him to go in. But he said to his father,

Reader 4: 'For years I have worked for you like a slave and have always obeyed you. But you have never even given me a little goat, so that I could give a dinner for my friends. This other son of yours wasted your money. And now that he has come home, you ordered the best calf to be killed for a feast.'

Reader 1: His father replied,

Reader 3: 'My son, you are always with me, and everything I have is yours. But we should be glad and celebrate! Your brother was dead, but he is now alive. He was lost and has now been found.'

Reader 1: The Gospel of the Lord.

All: Praise to you, Lord Jesus Christ.

Leader: Sometimes, we can act like the younger son, selfishly asking for anything we want, and then wasting it. At other times, we can act like the older son, refusing to forgive others who have hurt us. God, however, is always the loving Father, who patiently waits for us to say we are sorry, and then forgives us.

♪ *Play Reflective Music* (Track 22)

Close your eyes for a moment, and think about the answers to these questions. Be honest as you reflect on them. No-one will know the answers except you and God.

- Have you made time for God in your life; have you prayed every day?
- Have you made a special effort for God on Sundays by going to Mass?
- Have you done as your family and teachers ask?
- Have you been kind to your brothers, sisters and friends?
- Have you made people smile?
- Have you made people sad?
- Have you been lazy?
- Have you shared your things with others?
- Have you always told the truth?

- Have you borrowed things without returning them, or taken things that don't belong to you?

When you are ready, you can open your eyes.

We remember that God is like a loving father or mother. Just like the father in the story of the Prodigal Son, he is waiting for us to turn to him so that he can welcome us back.

If the Sacrament of Reconciliation is being celebrated as part of this service, now is the time for individual Confession and Absolution. If the Sacrament of Reconciliation is not being celebrated as part of this service, continue below.

Together, let us pray the Act of Sorrow, as a sign that we want to turn back to God:

All: O my God,
I thank you for loving me,
I am sorry for all my sins,
For not loving others and not loving you.
Help me to live like Jesus and not sin again.
Amen.

Leader: As a further sign that we want to continue our journey through Advent at peace with God and with one another, let us offer each other a sign of peace.

Children offer a sign of peace to those next to them

Leader: Let us pray:

Loving God,
We thank you for sending us your son, Jesus, to teach us about your love for us.
Help us to continue our preparations for Christmas at peace with you, and with each other.
We make this prayer through Christ our Lord.

All: Amen.

Leader: In the name of the Father, and of the Son and of the Holy Spirit.

All: Amen.

Closing Song: ♪ *Advent Hymn* (Track 1)

Term 1

12. Christmas (St Nicholas)

For the Leader: Christmas is a very special time in the lives of children. They are wide-eyed with excitement at all that this wonderful season has to offer them, from the joy of the Christmas story to the arrival of Santa. The person of Santa forms a large part of children's conversations at this time of year. The goodness of St Nicholas is to be found in the person of Santa. In this prayer service, your school community is invited to reflect on Saint Nicholas of Myra who lived in the fourth century. The Feast of St Nicholas is celebrated on December 6. He is the patron saint of children, brides and sailors.

You will need:
- Ten children to read
- Your school may be collecting gifts for an organisation that will distribute them to the families in need this Christmas. On the day that the students bring the gifts to school you could use the following prayer service. The gifts can be placed in the sacred space

Sacred Space:
- White cloth
- Bible
- Candle
- Cross/Crucifix
- Christmas Crib
- Image of St Nicholas
- Box wrapped in Christmas paper

Opening Song: ♪ *Come And Be Born In Our Hearts* (Track 11)

Leader: In the name of the Father, and of the Son and of the Holy Spirit.

All: Amen.

Leader: Let us begin with our Morning Prayer:

All: Father in heaven, you love me,
you are with me night and day.
I want to love you always
in all I do and say.
I'll try to please you, Father.
Bless me through the day. Amen.

Leader: As Christmas comes near, we hear a lot of talk about a man who wears a red outfit and has a white beard. We call him Santa Claus. We gather together today to remember another man who was very generous. He shared all that he had but people did not always know it was him who was doing it. His name was St Nicholas.

Reader 1: A long time ago, in Turkey, lived a man who loved God very much. His name was Nicholas. As he was growing up he was told about Jesus and he came to have a great love for God. While he was still young, a great sickness came to the place where he lived, and his mother and father both died. Nicholas then went to live with his uncle who was a bishop, where he learned even more about Jesus.

Reader 2: When Nicholas' parents died they were very rich, and now all this wealth was passed on to Nicholas. He decided that he had too much so he did as Jesus had asked in the Bible: he sold everything and gave it to people who were poor. The people were delighted, but they did not know who was helping them.

Reader 3: Early one morning, Nicholas arrived at the Church to pray. Many bishops were there too. They had come to pick a new bishop for a place called Myra. The night before, one of the older bishops had a dream that the first person who would arrive at the church that morning would be called Nicholas, and that he should be the new bishop. When the older bishop saw Nicholas and found out his name, it was decided: Nicholas became the Bishop of Myra.

Reader 4: Nicholas was a good bishop. He loved the people greatly, just as a shepherd cares for his sheep and as Jesus cares for us. Nicholas was especially kind to the poor and those who were in trouble. It is said that, at night, when people were asleep, he would go around and drop off food and other things to people so that they would not be hungry. St Nicholas lived and died more than a thousand years ago. After his death people called him Saint Nicholas.

Leader: Let us pray, asking God to help us to be as generous in our time and place as St Nicholas was in his. The response to each prayer is, 'Lord, help us to be generous'.

All: Lord, help us to be generous.

Reader 5: St Nicholas was kind to all the people. *(Response)*

Reader 6: St Nicholas followed the ways of Jesus in his life. *(Response)*

Reader 7: St Nicholas never asked for any reward for his generosity. *(Response)*

Reader 8: St Nicholas had a great love and care for the poor. *(Response)*

Reader 9: As we approach Christmas, may we think of those in the world who are not as lucky as we are. *(Response)*

Reader 10: May all children in the world know kindness and care. *(Response)*

Leader: Let us pray:

Loving God,
We thank you for the example St Nicholas, and his kindness to those in need.
Open our hearts in generosity to all who need our help.
We make this prayer through Christ our Lord.

All: Amen.

Leader: In the name of the Father, and of the Son and of the Holy Spirit.

All: Amen.

Closing Song: ♪ *Away In A Manger* (Track 4)

12. Christmas (St Nicholas)

Term 2

1. World Day of Peace

For the Leader: World Day of Peace is celebrated on January 1. January 1 is also the Solemnity of Mary, the Mother of God, whom we often refer to as 'Our Lady, Queen of Peace'. Every year, the Pope delivers a message for World Day of Peace. You might like to include an extract from this year's message as part of this prayer assembly. It can be found at www.vatican.va. As schools are on holidays on January 1, you can use this prayer service on the week when the children come back after the Christmas break.

> **You will need:**
> - Six children to read
>
> **Sacred Space:**
> - Green cloth
> - Bible, open at John 14:27
> - Candle
> - Cross/Crucifix
> - Statue or image of Mary
> - Rosary beads
> - Symbols of peace, such as doves

Opening Song: ♪ *Christ Is My Light* (Track 8)

Leader: In the name of the Father, and of the Son and of the Holy Spirit.

All: Amen.

Leader: Let us begin with a prayer to our Guardian Angel:

All: Angel sent by God to guide me,
be my light and walk beside me;
be my guardian and protect me;
on the paths of life direct me.
Amen.

Leader: We gather together today to pray for the gift of peace. On New Year's Day, people all over the world joined with our holy Father, the Pope, in praying for the gift of peace in the world. We know that Jesus left the world with his gift of peace. Let us listen to what he said:

Reader 1: *A reading from the Holy Gospel according to John (14:27)*
I give you peace, the kind of peace that only I can give. It isn't like the peace that this world can give. So don't be worried or afraid.

The Gospel of the Lord.

All: Praise to you, Lord Jesus Christ.

Leader: Sometimes, Jesus' gift of peace is not accepted. People argue and fight, and do not trust each other. We know that God's Holy Spirit helps people to bring God's peace to the world. Let us hear about some people who, with the help of God's Spirit, brought peace to the world.

Reader 2: For a long time, there was a war in Northern Ireland. People found it very hard to trust each other and to forgive each other. However, God's Spirit worked through the people and, slowly but surely, they found a way to live together in peace. On behalf of their communities, who fought against each other for a long time, John Hume and David Trimble were awarded the Nobel Peace Prize in 1998.

Reader 3: Nelson Mandela lived in South Africa at a time when the government believed that people should be separated based on the colour of their skin. Some people knew that this was wrong, because God creates all people equally. One of those people was Nelson Mandela. He suffered greatly because of his beliefs, and was even put in jail for no reason, but he forgave all those who mistreated him. He helped spread God's message of peace in South Africa.

Reader 4: After World War II ended in 1945, many countries decided that they needed to work together to make sure that there would never again be such a dreadful war. Fifty-one of these countries got together to form the United Nations. Countries who are part of the United Nations work together, help one another when help is needed, and try to make sure that peace reigns throughout the world. God's Spirit works through the United Nations, helping them to keep people in countries all over the world safe.

Leader: When we think of 'peace' we can sometimes think only about wars in far-off places, but in fact what we want is peace in our home, school and parish communities as well as in the whole world. Let us pray to God, asking that we might share the gift of peace with those in our world.

Reader 5: Help us to love one another

Reader 6: So that there can be peace in our homes.

Reader 5: Help us to share with one another

Reader 6: So that there can be peace in our school.

Reader 5: Help us to be kind to one another

Reader 6: So that there can be peace in our parish community.

Reader 5: Help us to show respect to those who are different

Reader 6: So that there can be peace in our country.

Reader 5: Help us to see things from the other person's point of view

Reader 6: So that there can be peace in our world.

Leader: Jesus left us the gift of peace. He also told us to call God 'our Father', and to pray for the gift of peace. That is why we dare to say:

All: Our Father .../Ár nAthair ...

Leader: As a sign of our willingness to bring the gift of peace to the world, let us offer each other a sign of peace.

Children offer a sign of peace to those next to them.

Leader: Let us finish with the Prayer for Peace, which we pray during each Mass:

Lord Jesus Christ, who said to your Apostles,
Peace I leave you, my peace I give you,
look not on our sins, but on the faith of your Church,
and graciously grant her peace and unity in accordance with your will.
Who live and reign for ever and ever.

All: Amen.

Leader: In the name of the Father, and of the Son and of the Holy Spirit.

All: Amen.

Closing Song: ♪ *Christ Be Our Light* (Track 7)

1. World Day of Peace

Term 2

2. Catholic Schools' Week

For the Leader: Organisations often take time to reflect on their identity. Doing so helps to strengthen their purposes and their vision, and to celebrate their achievements. Catholic Schools' Week gives us an opportunity to reflect on what it means to be a Catholic school, based on the mission and ministry of Jesus Christ. It also gives us the opportunity to celebrate the contribution that Catholic schools make to Irish society and to the mission of the Church.

Every year, Catholic Schools' Week has a different theme. You can find out about this year's focus at www.catholicbishops.ie/catholicschoolsweek.

> **You will need:**
> - Five children to read
> - One child to hold the candle
>
> **Sacred Space:**
> - Green cloth
> - Bible, open at Matthew 5:14-16
> - Candle
> - Candle stand or box on which the candle can be placed
> - Cross/Crucifix
> - School Crest
> - Image of school founder/foundress

Opening Song: ♪ *Christ Be Our Light* (Track 7)

Leader: In the name of the Father, and of the Son and of the Holy Spirit.

All: Amen.

Leader: Let us begin with a prayer to our Guardian Angel:

All: Angel sent by God to guide me,
be my light and walk beside me;
be my guardian and protect me;
on the paths of life direct me.
Amen.

Leader: We gather together today to celebrate Catholic Schools' Week. To be a Catholic School is something great, and if something is great, we need to tell everyone about it. In the Gospel reading, we hear how important it is to let your light shine so all can see it. Today, as we celebrate our Catholic School, we will shine our light of excellence, our light of joy, and our message of hope in Jesus, for all to see. Let us listen to the Gospel reading now:

As the Gospel is being proclaimed, invite a child to come forward to hold the candle. Light the candle, and ask the child to place it in the sacred space. Elevate it slightly, if possible, using a candle stand or box.

Reader 1: *A reading from the Holy Gospel according to Matthew (5:14-16)*
You are like light for the whole world. A city built on top of a hill cannot be hidden, and no one would light a lamp and put it under a clay pot. A lamp is placed on a lampstand, where it can give light to everyone in the house. Make your light shine, so that others will see the good that you do and will praise your Father in heaven.

The Gospel of the Lord.

All: Praise to you, Lord Jesus Christ.

Leader: Jesus wants us to let our light shine, so that others will see it, and will thank God for us. Here at _____ school, we try our best to let our light shine. We shine in _____ (*name some of the things in which your school excels*). Let us pray to God in thanksgiving for all those who help us to let our light shine for all to see. The response to each prayer is, 'Lord, graciously hear us'.

All: Lord, graciously hear us.

Reader 2: We pray for our parents, who are our most important teachers. May they continue to pass on their light of faith to us. Lord, hear us. (*Response*)

Reader 3: We pray for our teachers, who help us to see the ways in which we can let our light shine. Lord, hear us. *(Response)*

Reader 4: We pray for our Board of Management, caretaker, secretary, cleaners, Special Needs assistants, and all who help to make our school a great place to be. We thank them for sharing their light with us. Lord, hear us. *(Response)*

Reader 5: We pray that all who come to learn and work in this Catholic School may feel the light of your love. Lord, hear us. *(Response)*

Leader: We take a moment to remember any special prayer we may have in our hearts today. Lord, hear us. *(Response)*

Let us pray:

Jesus, our friend,
As you grew you became wise.
May all who come to this Catholic School grow in wisdom and love for you.
May they grow to be the best person they possibly can be, letting their light shine for all to see.
We make this prayer through Christ our Lord.

All: Amen.

Leader: In the name of the Father, and of the Son and of the Holy Spirit.

All: Amen.

Closing Song: ♪ *Community Song* (Track 12)

2. Catholic Schools' Week

Term 2

3. St Brigid

For the Leader: St Brigid's Day is celebrated on February 1. St Brigid is said to have been born at Faughart in County Louth, but she eventually settled in County Kildare, where she built a church and convent, which exists to this day. While she is revered for many things, including her care for those who were sick and poor, the focus on this prayer assembly will be on St Brigid's commitment to prayer, emphasised through the establishment of her church.

> **You will need:**
> - Nine children to read
>
> **Sacred Space:**
> - Green cloth
> - Bible
> - Candle
> - St Brigid's Cross/Crucifix
> - Holy Water
> - Some spring flowers, signifying the traditional beginning of springtime on St Brigid's Day

Opening Song: ♪ *Christ Be Beside Me* (Track 6)

Leader: In the name of the Father, and of the Son and of the Holy Spirit.

All: Amen.

Leader: Let us begin with a prayer to our Guardian Angel:

All: Angel sent by God to guide me,
be my light and walk beside me;
be my guardian and protect me;
on the paths of life direct me.
Amen.

Leader: We gather together today on the Feast of St Brigid. St Brigid lived around the time of St Patrick. She was born in County Louth. She was a kind woman, who spent her life helping other people. Let us listen to a story about St Brigid.*

Reader 1: Brigid and her friends wanted to tell all the people in the land about the love of God. They wanted everyone to hear the Good News that God loved them. Brigid decided she must build a church, so that everyone would have a place to come when they wanted to talk to God. But Brigid had no land on which to build her church.

Reader 2: 'Someone will have to give me land on which to build my church. I will go to the chieftain and ask him for a piece of ground.'

Reader 1: And off she went. Now the chieftain was a very sly man. He did not know anything about God's love and he did not want to listen to Brigid. He decided he would play a trick on her. When Brigid asked the chieftain for some land on which to build her church, he said,

Reader 3: 'Very well. Come with me.'

Reader 1: He took Brigid to the top of a high hill.

Reader 3: 'Look down there. All the land, as far as you can see, is mine. It belongs to me.'

Reader 1: Then he told Brigid to take off her cloak.

Reader 3: 'You asked me for land. I will give you as much land as your cloak can cover. Take it off and lay it down on the ground and see how much ground it covers.'

Reader 1: Brigid was very disappointed. She knew her cloak was very small and would not cover nearly enough land to build a church. The chieftain laughed

---
* Taken from *Alive-O 1*, p. 135.

and laughed. Brigid laid her cloak on the ground. You would hardly believe was happened next. The cloak began to grow bigger and bigger. It spread our wider and wider, further and further. The chieftain stopped laughing. His face grew pale. The cloak was still growing.

Reader 3: 'Stop it! Stop it, please! Stop it quickly! Stop it now!'

Reader 1: Now it was Brigid's turn to laugh. She told the cloak to stop. She had more than enough land now to build her church. She went back and told her friends what had happened. That night they thanked God for helping them with their church.

Leader: St Brigid knew how important it is to pray to God. We also know how important it is to pray to God. That's why we gather together here, in _____ school, today. Let us ask St Brigid to help us to pray to God at all times, in our homes, in our school, and in our parish Church. The response to each prayer is, 'St Brigid, pray for us.'

All: St Brigid, pray for us.

Reader 4: When we gather together here in _____ school to pray to God, we ask St Brigid to guide us. *(Response)*

Reader 5: When we gather at Mass to pray to God, we ask St Brigid to guide us. *(Response)*

Reader 6: When we pray to God at home, we ask St Brigid to guide us. *(Response)*

Reader 7: When we pray quietly in our minds, using our inside voices, we ask St Brigid to guide us. *(Response)*

Reader 8: When we pray by singing out loud, we ask St Brigid to guide us. *(Response)*

Reader 9: When we pray by moving our bodies, we ask St Brigid to guide us. *(Response)*

Leader: Together, let us give glory to God, just as St Brigid did:

All: Glory be to the Father .../*Glóir don Athair* ...

Leader: Let us pray:

Loving God,
We thank you for the life of Brigid, a great Irish saint.
Bless our homes, schools, churches, and all places where we pray.
Help us to show our love for you, just like St Brigid did.
We make this prayer through Christ our Lord.

All: Amen.

Leader: In the name of the Father, and of the Son and of the Holy Spirit.

All: Amen.

Closing Song: ♪ *We Sing A Song To Brigid* (Track 34)

3. St Brigid

Term 2

4. Our Lady of Lourdes/World Day of the Sick

For the Leader: The Feast of Our Lady of Lourdes is celebrated on February 11. This feast day celebrates the appearance of the Blessed Virgin Mary to Bernadette Soubirous, a fourteen-year-old girl, in Lourdes, France. Mary told Bernadette to dig in the ground until she found a spring of water. Today, millions of pilgrims from all over the world travel to Lourdes to wash in the water from that spring and to pray for healing. Many confirmed miracles have been attributed to Our Lady of Lourdes, through the intercession of St Bernadette. In 1993, Blessed Pope John Paul II named the Feast of Our Lady of Lourdes as the World Day of the Sick. He asked that on this day, we pray with and for those who are sick and suffering, and those who care for them. If there is anyone in your school community who is sick at this time, you can name them specifically during this prayer service.

You will need:
- One prayer card for each person. The template for this card is on page 51. These should be completed before the prayer assembly begins, and gathered up in baskets or small containers. These baskets or containers will be brought to the sacred space during the service
- One child from each class to carry the basket or container to the sacred space
- Six children to read

Sacred Space:
- White or blue cloth
- Bible, open at Mark 2:1-12
- Candle
- Cross/Crucifix
- Statue or image of Mary
- Rosary beads
- Holy Water
- Symbols of healing, such as a First Aid kit, bandages, plasters, empty medicine bottles etc.

Opening Song: ♪ *Magnificat* (Track 19)

Leader: In the name of the Father, and of the Son and of the Holy Spirit.

All: Amen.

Leader: Let us begin with a prayer to our Guardian Angel:

All: Angel sent by God to guide me,
be my light and walk beside me;
be my guardian and protect me;
on the paths of life direct me.
Amen.

Leader: We gather together today to pray for people who are sick, and those who care for them. Millions of people, all over the world, are doing the same thing, because today is the World Day of the Sick. Many of us know someone who is sick. We will pray for them in a special way today. Let us begin by listening to a story from the Gospel according to Mark. It is about how Jesus healed a man who could not walk.

Reader 1: *A reading from the Holy Gospel according to Mark (2:1-5, 11-12)*
Jesus went back to Capernaum, and a few days later people heard that he was at home. Then so many of them came to the house that there wasn't even standing room left in front of the door. Jesus was still teaching when four people came up, carrying a crippled man on a mat. But because of the crowd, they could not get him to Jesus. So they made a hole in the roof above him and let the man down in front of everyone. When Jesus saw how much faith they had, he said to the crippled man, 'My friend, your sins are forgiven. Get up! Pick up your mat and go on home.' The man got right up. He picked up his mat and went out while everyone watched in amazement. They praised God and said, 'We have never seen anything like this!'

The Gospel of the Lord

All: Praise to you, Lord Jesus Christ.

Leader: Because Jesus was God's only Son, he had the power to heal people who were sick. Can you think of any other people that Jesus healed? *(Invite children to think in silence or to answer aloud, whichever is most appropriate.)*

We cannot heal people the way Jesus did. However, there are people, like nurses, doctors and volunteers, who take care of people who are sick, and sometimes those sick people are healed. We can also help people who are sick by praying for them, and that's what we want to do today. I know that everyone has filled out a prayer card, on which you have written the names of people you know who are sick. We will now bring these names and place them in our sacred space, and we will ask God to bless these people in a special way today.

You can organise the bringing forward of the names in a way that best suits the size of your school. The following is a suggestion of how it might be done. (Pause after each sentence, to allow time for the names to be carried to the sacred space)

Reader 2:
_____ brings the names of the people that Junior Infants want to pray for.
_____ brings the names of the people that Senior Infants want to pray for.
_____ brings the names of the people that 1st class(es) want to pray for.
_____ brings the names of the people that 2nd class(es) want to pray for.
_____ brings the names of the people that 3rd class(es) want to pray for.
_____ brings the names of the people that 4th class(es) want to pray for.
_____ brings the names of the people that 5th class(es) want to pray for.
_____ brings the names of the people that 6th class(es) want to pray for.

Leader: Close your eyes for a moment, and think about the person you want to pray for. Try to see their picture in your head. Ask God to bless them in a special way today. *(Pause)*

When you are ready, you can open your eyes. Together, let us offer our prayers to God. The response to each prayer is 'Jesus, the healer, hear our prayer.'

All: Jesus, the healer, hear our prayer.

Reader 3: We pray for people who are sick. May God bless them in a special way today. *(Response)*

Reader 4: We pray for people who look after those who are sick at home. May God help them to continue to show love to others. *(Response)*

Reader 5: We pray for nurses, doctors, and all who look after those who are in hospital. May God bless their good work. *(Response)*

Reader 6: We pray for people who are sick all over the world, and who have no one to care for them. May they know that God is with them. *(Response)*

Leader: We often ask Mary to pray for people who are sick. This is because some people have been cured when they visited holy places where Mary appeared. One of these places is called Lourdes, and it is in France. Someone you know may have visited Lourdes. Many people go there to ask Mary to help them to get better. Today is the Feast of Our Lady of Lourdes so, together, let us pray:

All: Hail Mary …/'Sé do bheatha, a Mhuire …

Leader: Let us pray:

Loving God,
We thank you for the gift of our good health.
May we always use our good health to help other people.
Bless those who are sick. May they feel your healing presence at this time.
We make this prayer through Christ our Lord.

All: Amen.

Leader: In the name of the Father, and of the Son and of the Holy Spirit.

All: Amen.

Closing Song: ♪ *Mary, Our Mother* (Track 20)

4. Our Lady of Lourdes/World Day of the Sick

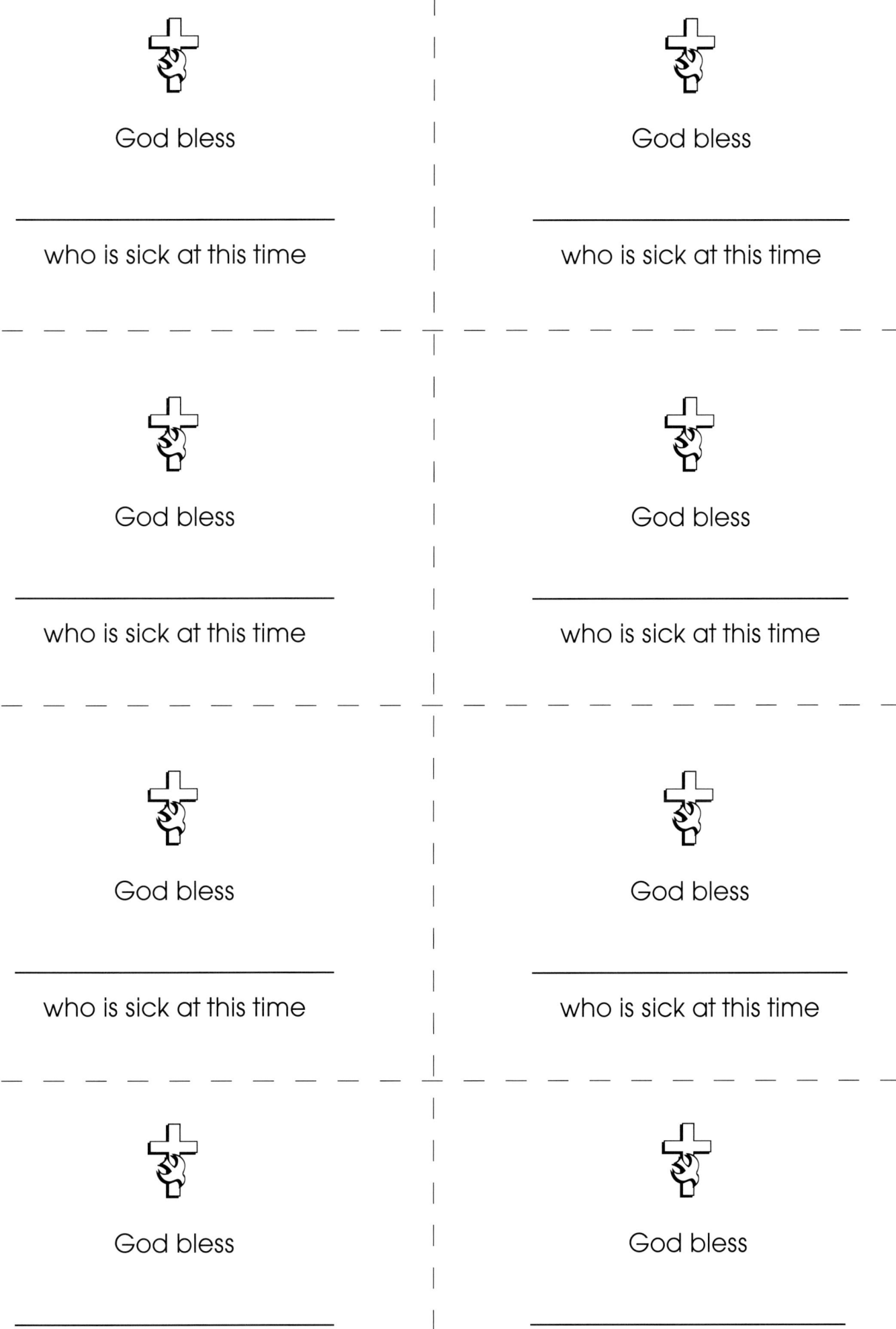

51

Term 2

5. St Valentine

For the Leader: St Valentine's Day is celebrated on February 14. Much is unclear about the life of this third-century saint, but we do know that he was a martyr who died for his faith. What we can be sure of, then, is that he lived his life based on the Gospel message of love. Today, his memory tends to be celebrated more as a romantic holiday rather than as a Christian memorial. This prayer service therefore focuses on the religious meaning of St Valentine's Day, and how we can share God's love in our home, school and parish communities today.

> **You will need:**
> - Four children to read
>
> **Sacred Space:**
> - Red cloth
> - Bible, open at John 4:11-16
> - Candle
> - Cross/Crucifix
> - Image of St Valentine

Opening Song: ♪ *This Is The Day* (Track 30)

Leader: In the name of the Father, and of the Son and of the Holy Spirit.

All: Amen.

Leader: Let us begin with a prayer to our Guardian Angel:

All: Angel sent by God to guide me,
be my light and walk beside me;
be my guardian and protect me;
on the paths of life direct me.
Amen.

Leader: We gather together today to reflect on the life of St Valentine, who lived in Rome about two hundred years after Jesus died. When we think about St Valentine's Day, we often just think about giving cards and gifts to the people we love. There is much more to learn from St Valentine, however. Let us listen to the story of his life:

Reader 1: Legend has it that St Valentine lived at the time of the Roman Emperor Claudius II. Claudius II fought a lot of wars in his attempt to spread the Roman Empire, and so he needed lots of soldiers for his armies. Claudius believed that men who were not married made the best soldiers, because they didn't have anyone to worry about except themselves. So, he did not allow his soldiers to marry, and threatened to throw them in jail or even have them killed if they disobeyed him.

Reader 2: Many of the soldiers in Claudius' army wanted to be married, however. St Valentine heard about their dilemma, and arranged to meet the soldiers and their fiancés privately. Valentine knew that his life would be in danger if he was caught, but he was inspired by the love that the couples had for each other. He married the couples who came to him in secret, going against the Emperor's orders.

Reader 3: The news that there was a priest who was willing to marry the soldiers and their fiancés soon spread not only to the army, but to the rest of Rome, and to the Emperor Claudius. St Valentine was arrested and we know that he was eventually killed because he refused to give up his belief in God. St Valentine knew that the love between a couple was like the love God has for all of us, and he could never deny that.

Leader: Let us listen to a passage from the Gospel, which no doubt influenced the life of St Valentine.

Reader 4: *A reading from the first letter of St John (4:11-12, 16)*
Dear friends, since God loved us this much, we must love each other. No one has ever seen God. But if we

love each other, God lives in us, and his love is truly in our hearts. God is love. If we keep on loving others, we will stay one in our hearts with God, and he will stay one with us.

The Word of the Lord.

All: Thanks be to God.

Leader: John tells us that '… since God loved us this much, we must love each other.' Let us therefore decide that today, on St Valentine's Day, we will show our friends, families and neighbours that we care for and love them. In this way, we will bring God to them. As a sign of our love for one another, let us offer each other a sign of peace.

Children offer a sign of peace to those next to them

Leader: Let us pray the Act of Love together:

If children are not familiar with the Act of Love, read it line-by-line and invite them to repeat it after you.

All: O my God,
I love you with all my heart, with all my soul, and with all my strength.
Lord, increase our love.
Help us to love one another.

Leader: Let us pray:

Loving God,
We thank you for the example of St Valentine.
He was courageous in his faith, and never gave up his belief in your love for all people.
Help us to be like him in all things, and to share your love with one another today and always.
We make this prayer through Christ our Lord.

All: Amen.

Leader: In the name of the Father, and of the Son and of the Holy Spirit.

All: Amen.

Closing Song: ♪ *Circle Of Friends* (Track 9)

5. St Valentine

Term 2

6. Ash Wednesday

For the Leader: Ash Wednesday is the first day of the liturgical season of Lent. On Ash Wednesday, ashes are worn as a sign of our willingness to repent. These ashes are made from the ash of the burnt, blessed palms from Palm Sunday of the previous year. In generations past, people were encouraged to abstain from meat for the whole of the Lenten season. Today, there are only two days of fasting and abstinence: Ash Wednesday and Good Friday. Fasting means that the amount of food we eat is considerably reduced. Abstinence means that we give up particular kinds of food or drink, for example meat and alcohol. Children and those who are elderly are exempt from fasting.

> **You will need:**
> - Eight children to read
> - Three children to carry symbols to the sacred space
>
> **Sacred Space:**
> - Violet cloth
> - Bible, open at Matthew 4:1-11
> - Candle
> - Cross/Crucifix
> - A wilderness space containing some sand, twigs and stones
> - Other items will be added to the sacred space during the service: a Trócaire Box, a prayer book and some sweets
> - Ashes, if they are to be distributed

Opening Song: ♪ *Wilderness* (Track 35)

Leader: In the name of the Father, and of the Son and of the Holy Spirit.

All: Amen.

Leader: Let us begin with a prayer to our Guardian Angel:

All: Angel sent by God to guide me,
be my light and walk beside me;
be my guardian and protect me;
on the paths of life direct me.
Amen.

Leader: We gather together today to celebrate Ash Wednesday. Ash Wednesday is the first day in the season of Lent. During Lent we remember that Jesus spent forty days in the wilderness, praying and fasting. Let us hear about his time there.

Reader 1: *A reading from the Holy Gospel according to Matthew (4:1-11)*
The Holy Spirit led Jesus into the desert, so that the devil could test him. After Jesus had gone without eating for forty days and nights, he was very hungry. Then the devil came to him and said,

Reader 2: 'If you are God's Son, tell these stones to turn into bread.'

Reader 1: Jesus answered,

Reader 3: The Scriptures say: "No one can live only on food. People need every word that God has spoken."'

Reader 1: Next, the devil took Jesus to the holy city and had him stand on the highest part of the temple. The devil said,

Reader 2: 'If you are God's Son, jump off. The Scriptures say: "God will give his angels orders about you. They will catch you in their arms, and you won't hurt your feet on the stones."'

Reader 1: Jesus answered,

Reader 3: The Scriptures also say, "Don't try to test the Lord your God!"'

Reader 1: Finally, the devil took Jesus up on a very high mountain and showed him all the kingdoms on earth and their power. The devil said to him,

Reader 2: 'I will give all this to you, if you will bow down and worship me.'

Reader 1: Jesus answered,

Reader 3: 'Go away Satan! The Scriptures say: "Worship the Lord your God and serve only him."'

Reader 1: Then the devil left Jesus, and angels came to help him.

The Gospel of the Lord.

All: Praise to you, Lord Jesus Christ.

Leader: What Jesus did in the wilderness was very difficult. But he did not give up. As his followers, we want to follow his example during the season of Lent, and so we often make Lenten promises. But what promises should we make?

♪ *Play Reflective Music* (Track 22)

Reader 2: Our first promise should be to pray more than we usually do. *(Pause)*

Child holds up a prayer book and places it in the sacred space.

When will you pray? In the morning, on your way to school? In the afternoon, on your way home from school? At night, before you go to bed? Make your promise now, and ask God to help you. *(Pause)*

Reader 3: Our second promise should be to go without, or abstain from, something, like sweets or chocolate, or playing video games.

Child holds up some sweets and places them in the sacred space.

What will you abstain from? Is there something you like, but that you could do without? Make your promise now, and ask God to help you. *(Pause)*

Reader 4: Our third promise should be to give alms or to be charitable. Being charitable means using what we have to help people who are in need.

Child holds up a Trócaire box and places it in the sacred space.

Do you have a Trócaire box in your house? Can you put some money in it during Lent? Are there other ways that you can share with people who are in need? Make your promise now, and ask God to help you. *(Pause)*

Leader: It can be difficult to do all of these things, but we know that Jesus is there to help us, and we can support each other. Let us pray for the strength to turn away from sin, and to be faithful to the Gospel during these Lenten days. The response to each prayer is, 'Jesus in the wilderness, help us.'

All: Jesus in the wilderness, help us.

Reader 5: That we may turn away from sin and be faithful to the Gospel. *(Response)*

Reader 6: That we may remember that we are always in need of God's forgiveness. *(Response)*

Reader 7: That we may be strong enough to keep our Lenten promises. *(Response)*

Reader 8: Jesus in the wilderness,
in those moments when we choose to do without and find it difficult, help us, strengthen us with thoughts of others who do without and have no choice.*

If ashes are being distributed as part of this service, now is the time to do so. If ashes are not being distributed as part of this prayer assembly, continue below.

Leader: Jesus, our friend,
As we make this Lenten journey, may we turn away from sin and be faithful to the Gospel.
May our eyes be open to the needs of others.
May our ears be open to their call and to your Word.
May our hearts be open to care for each other and to welcome you into our lives.
We make this prayer through Christ our Lord.

All: Amen.

Leader: In the name of the Father, and of the Son and of the Holy Spirit.

All: Amen.

Closing Song: ♪ *The Way To Be* (Track 28)

---
* *Alive-O 6,* Poster.

6. Ash Wednesday

Term 2

7. Mother's Day

For the Leader: Mother's Day is the perfect time to encourage children to pray for their mothers, grandmothers, godmothers, and other women who help to take care of them. We also ask Mary, the Mother of the Church, to pray for all mothers. You may need to be sensitive to any children who have been bereaved or separated from the women who care for them.

> **You will need:**
> - Six children to read
> - Baskets/small containers containing the required number of Mother's Day prayers for each child to take home. You can distribute these as children leave the prayer assembly area
> - Children to hold the baskets/containers
>
> **Sacred Space:**
> - White or blue cloth
> - Bible, open at John 2:1-11
> - Candle
> - Cross/Crucifix
> - Statue of image of Mary
> - Rosary beads

Opening Song: ♪ *Magnificat* (Track 19)

Leader: In the name of the Father, and of the Son and of the Holy Spirit.

All: Amen.

Leader: Let us begin with a prayer to our Guardian Angel:

All: Angel sent by God to guide me,
be my light and walk beside me;
be my guardian and protect me;
on the paths of life direct me.
Amen.

Leader: We gather together today to celebrate Mother's Day, and to thank God for our mothers/mammies, our grandmothers/grannies, our godmothers and any other women who are like a mother to us. Let us begin by listening to a story about Mary and Jesus.

Reader 1: *A reading from the Holy Gospel according to John* (2:1-11)
Three days later Mary, the mother of Jesus, was at a wedding feast in the village of Cana in Galilee. Jesus and his disciples had also been invited and were there. When the wine was all gone, Mary said to Jesus, 'They don't have any more wine.' Jesus replied, 'Mother, my time hasn't yet come: you must not tell me what to do.' Mary then said to the servants, 'Do whatever Jesus tells you to do.'

At the feast there were six stone water jars that were used by the people for washing themselves in the way that their religion said they must. Each jar held about twenty or thirty gallons. Jesus told the servants to fill them to the top with water. Then after the jars had been filled, he said, 'Now take some water and give it to the man in charge of the feast.'

The servants did as Jesus told them, and the man in charge drank some of the water that had now turned into wine. He did not know where the wine had come from, but the servants did. He called the bridegroom over and said, 'The best wine is always served first. Then after the guests have had plenty, the other wine is served. But you have kept the best until last!'

This was Jesus' first miracle, and he did it in the village of Cana in Galilee. There Jesus showed his glory, and his disciples put their faith in him.

The Gospel of the Lord.

All: Praise to you, Lord Jesus Christ.

Leader: This was Jesus' first ever miracle. Who was it that told him to help the bride and groom? Who told him to perform this miracle? *(Invite children to think in silence or to answer aloud, whichever is most appropriate)*

It was Mary who told Jesus that it was time for him to show the world that he was God's Son. At first, Jesus didn't want to do it. Sometimes, our mothers/mammies can ask us to do things that we don't want to do either. It might be to tidy our room, or help our younger brothers or sisters, or even to go to bed! Jesus knew that his mother was trying to help him to do the right thing, and so he did as she asked. We are also trying to do the right thing, and trying to live like Jesus. That's why we should also do as our mothers/mammies ask us.

Mother's Day is an opportunity for us to say 'Thank You' to our mothers/mammies, grandmothers/grannies, godmothers, and any other women who are like a mother to us. We ask God to bless them, and to help them to take good care of us. Let us offer our prayers to God now. The response to each prayer is, 'Lord, hear our prayer'.

All: Lord, hear our prayer.

Reader 2: We pray for all mothers. May God be with them as they care for their children. We pray to the Lord. *(Response)*

Reader 3: We pray for all women who are pregnant at this time. May God help them to deliver their babies safely. We pray to the Lord. *(Response)*

Reader 4: We pray for people whose mothers have died. May they know that their mothers are safe in heaven with God. We pray to the Lord. *(Response)*

Reader 5: We pray for our grannies. May we always show them how much we love them. We pray to the Lord. *(Response)*

Reader 6: We pray for our godmothers. May they help us to get to know God better. We pray to the Lord. *(Response)*

Leader: Together, let us pray:

All: Hail Mary .../ 'Sé do bheatha, a Mhuire ...

Leader: Let us pray:

Loving God,
We thank you for our mothers/mammies, grandmothers/grannies, godmothers, and any other women who are like a mother to us.
Bless them on Mother's Day. Help us to show our love for them on that day and on all days.
We make this prayer through Christ our Lord.

All: Amen.

Leader: As you leave, you will receive a 'Prayer for Mothers'. When you get back to your classroom, take some time to decorate it. On Mother's Day, give it to someone you love, and tell them that you have been praying for them.

In the name of the Father, and of the Son and of the Holy Spirit.

All: Amen.

Closing Song: ♪ *Mary, Our Mother* (Track 20)

7. Mother's Day

 God bless you this Mother's Day

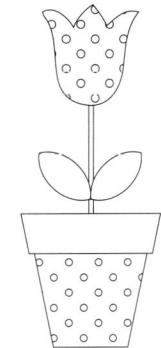 God bless you this Mother's Day

 God bless you this Mother's Day

 God bless you this Mother's Day

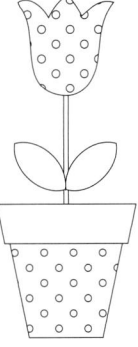 God bless you this Mother's Day

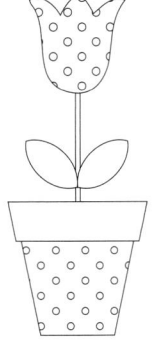 God bless you this Mother's Day

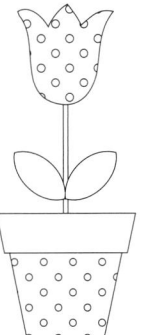 God bless you this Mother's Day

 God bless you this Mother's Day

Term 2

8. Lent, focusing on the work of Trócaire

For the Leader: Trócaire is the official overseas development agency of the Catholic Church in Ireland. It was set up by the Irish Catholic Bishops in 1973 to express the concern of the Irish Church for the suffering of the world's poorest and most oppressed people. Today, Trócaire works in thirty-eight countries in Africa, Asia, Latin America and the Middle East. Their programmes aim to:
- Build a sustainable way of life and help people cope with climate change
- Respond to emergencies and disasters
- Tackle injustice and defend human rights
- Address the HIV and AIDS crisis
- Support gender equality

Every year, Trócaire's Lenten campaign concentrates on a different issue. You can find out about the focus of this year's campaign at www.trocaire.org.

You will need:
- Six readers
- Five children to carry symbols to the sacred space

Sacred Space:
- Violet cloth
- Bible, open at Luke 10:25-37
- Candle
- Cross/Crucifix
- A wilderness space containing some sand, twigs and stones
- A Trócaire box
- A globe
- Other items will be added to the sacred space during the service: a hammer, bread, a First Aid kit and the two pictures from pages 62 and 63 of this book

Opening Song: ♪ *Whatsoever You Do* (Track 32)

Leader: In the name of the Father, and of the Son and of the Holy Spirit.

All: Amen.

Leader: Let us begin with a prayer to our Guardian Angel:

All: Angel sent by God to guide me,
be my light and walk beside me;
be my guardian and protect me;
on the paths of life direct me.
Amen.

Leader: We gather together today to continue our journey through Lent. During the forty days of Lent, we try our best to do three things: firstly, to pray more than we usually do; secondly, to go without, or abstain from, something, like sweets, or playing video games; and thirdly, to be charitable. Being charitable means using what we have to help people who are in need. But who should we help? A man asked Jesus a very similar question one day. The man was an expert in the Law of Moses. He knew that the Law of Moses tells us to love God and to love our neighbour. But his question to Jesus was, 'Who is my neighbour?' Jesus told a story to help him to understand. Let us listen to that story now.

Reader 1: *A reading from the Holy Gospel according to Luke (10:25-37)*
Jesus said: 'A man was going down from Jerusalem to Jericho, when he was attacked by robbers. They stripped him of his clothes, beat him and went away, leaving him half dead. A priest happened to be going down the same road, and when he saw the man, he passed by on the other side. So too, a Levite, when he came to the place and saw him, passed by on the other side. But a Samaritan, as he travelled, came where the man was; and when he saw him, he took pity on him. He went to him and bandaged his wounds, pouring on oil and wine. Then he put the man on his own donkey, brought him to an inn and took care of him. The next day he took out two denarii and gave them to the innkeeper. "Look after him," he said, "and when I return, I will reimburse you for any extra expense you may have." Which of these three do you think was a neighbour to the man who fell into the

hands of robbers?' Jesus asked. The expert in the law replied, 'The one who had mercy on him.' Jesus told him, 'Go and do likewise.'

The Gospel of the Lord.

All: Praise to you, Lord Jesus Christ.

Leader: The Samaritan was a good neighbour to the man who was attacked. But the thing is, Jews and Samaritans were not neighbours at all. In fact, they were often enemies. They did not live close to each other, and sometimes did not even speak to each other. So, when Jesus told us this story, he was not only telling us to help people we know and who live close to us; he was telling us to help people anywhere and everywhere who need it.

One group of people who act like the Good Samaritan are the people who work for Trócaire. Trócaire is an Irish word that means 'Mercy'. Trócaire works with people in countries which are still growing and developing, and where people do not have as much as we have. Let's listen to some of the activities that Trócaire are involved in:

Reader 2: Trócaire responds to help people caught in emergencies such as earthquakes and floods. They help people to rebuild their houses, schools and hospitals, and to build all these things in a better way so that they will not be destroyed again.

Child holds up a hammer and places it in the sacred space

Reader 3: Some governments and businesses do not treat their people with respect. Trócaire makes sure that the people's voices are heard. They work on behalf of people who are being mistreated to make sure that they have a right to vote, that they are treated fairly and that they are paid a fair wage.

Child holds up the picture of a speech bubble and places it in the sacred space

Reader 4: Trócaire works to build peace in the countries where wars are going on, or where wars have just ended. It is very difficult for people to trust each other when they have been fighting. Trócaire helps them to see that everyone must work together if things are going to be better.

Child holds up the picture of people shaking hands and places it in the sacred space

Reader 5: Trócaire supports people who have a blood disease called HIV by providing treatment programmes to help those who are sick in Asia, Africa and Latin America. Trócaire also helps people to understand how they can catch diseases, and tries to stop them spreading.

Child holds up a First Aid kit and places it in the sacred space

Reader 6: Today, one in six people do not have enough food to live a healthy life. Trócaire doesn't just give people the food they need. Trócaire helps families to develop the best ways of farming and of storing food, to make sure that they will always have enough to eat.

Child holds up some bread and places it in the sacred space

Leader: Jesus told us that we should act like the Good Samaritan; that is, we should act with kindness and generosity when there is someone who needs help. This is exactly what Trócaire does. Every Lent, we receive a Trócaire box. This box reminds us to help those who are in need, and to do so in a special way during Lent. When we put money in the Trócaire box, it goes straight to those who need it. So, as we give to Trócaire, we are also acting like the Good Samaritan in the story.

Let us pray:

Loving God,
We thank you for the opportunity to help those who are in need.
Bless the work of Trócaire, and help us to share generously with them during this season of Lent.
May we always act like Good Samaritans, following the example given to us by Jesus, who is our teacher and friend.
We make this prayer through Christ our Lord.

All: Amen.

Leader: In the name of the Father, and of the Son and of the Holy Spirit.

All: Amen.

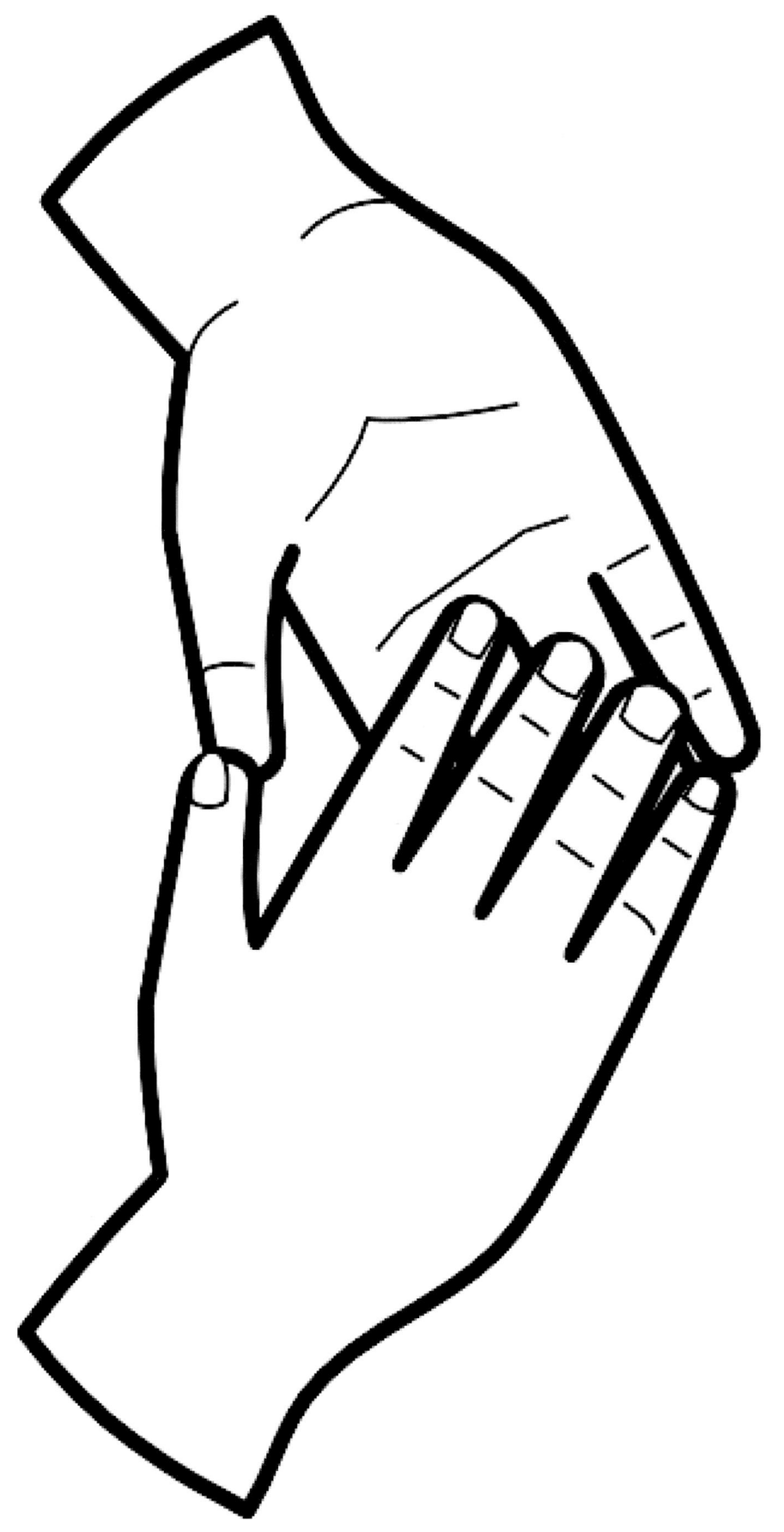

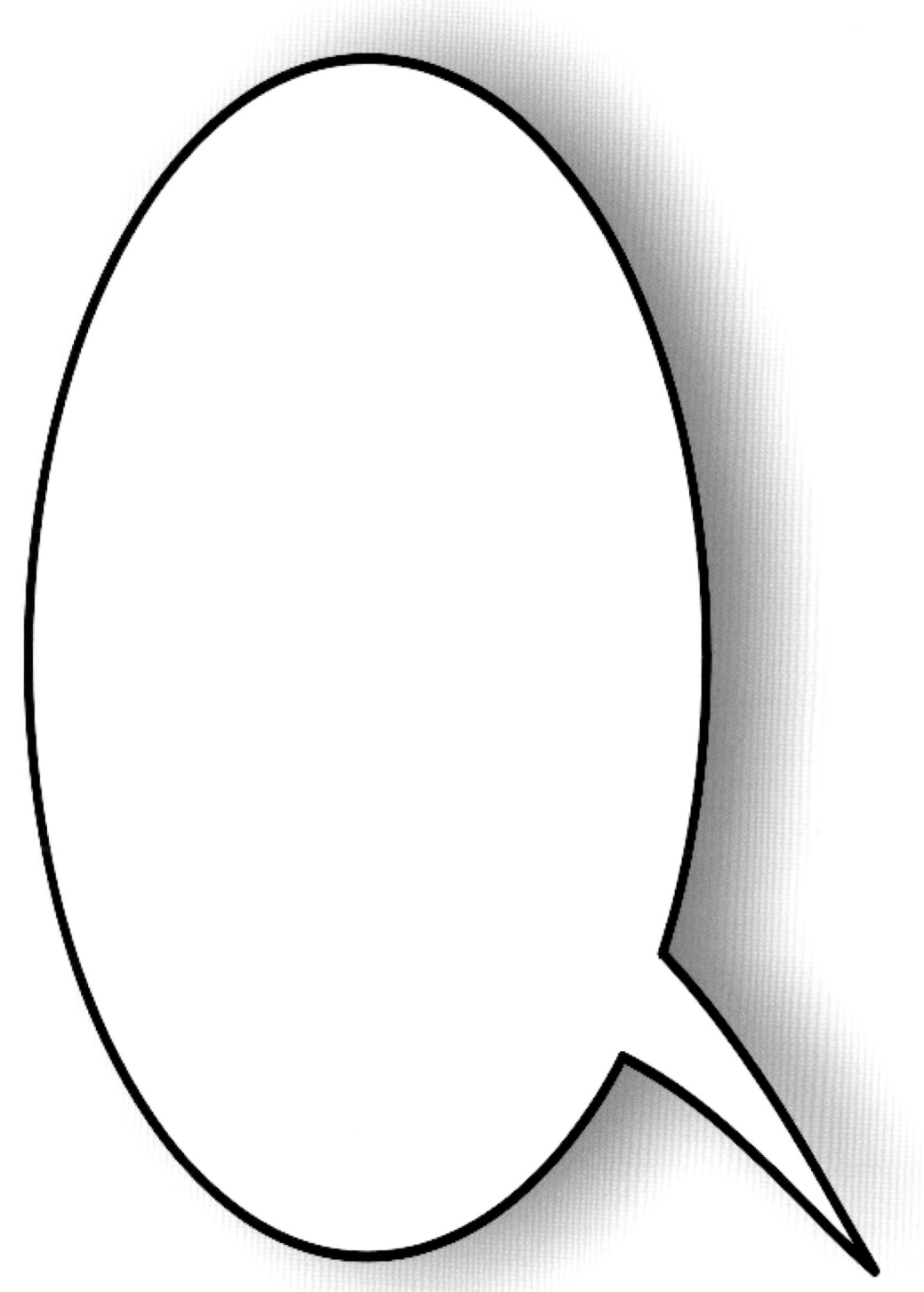

Term 2

9. St Patrick

For the Leader: The Feast of St Patrick is celebrated on March 17. On this day Irish people across the world celebrate their Irishness, with music and language, and through their faith and customs. St Patrick was born in Wales and was brought to Ireland as a slave at about the age of sixteen. After six years he managed to escape and returned home. Later in life, he became a priest and then a bishop, and eventually returned to Ireland to spread the Christian faith here. Most of what we know about Patrick today comes from his *Confessions* and *Letters to Coroticus*.

> **You will need:**
> - Nine children to read
> - Five children to carry symbols to the sacred space
> - If you have a traditional group of musicians in the school they may wish to play as part of this prayer assembly
>
> **Sacred Space:**
> - White or green cloth
> - Bible
> - Candle
> - Image of St Patrick
> - Holy water
> - Other items will be added to the sacred space during the service: a cross/crucifix and the four pictures from pages 66 and 67 of this book

Opening Song: ♪ *Christ Be Beside Me* (Track 6)

Leader: In the name of the Father, and of the Son and of the Holy Spirit.

All: Amen.

Leader: Let us begin with a prayer to our Guardian Angel:

All: Angel sent by God to guide me,
be my light and walk beside me;
be my guardian and protect me;
on the paths of life direct me.
Amen.

Leader: We gather together today to reflect on the life of St Patrick, who brought the Christian faith to Ireland many years ago. Let us learn about his life:

Reader 1: St Patrick was born in Wales around 389 AD. His father was a Christian and was a deacon in his local church. Patrick did not make much time in his life for prayer and getting to know God, as he was too busy going to school and doing other things. In his book called *Confessions*, which he wrote near the end of his life, he said, 'I did not, indeed, know the true God.'

Child holds up the picture of the date 389 AD and places it in the sacred space

Reader 2: At the age of sixteen, St Patrick was captured by Vikings and taken to Ireland where he was sold as a slave. He was bought by a man named Milchu. Milchu was an Irish chieftain. St Patrick was sent to work minding pigs and sheep on a mountain called Slemish in County Antrim.

Child holds up the picture of sheep and places it in the sacred space

Reader 3: This was a very lonely time in St Patrick's life and he turned to God in prayer. He wrote, 'I used to stay out in the forests and on the mountain and I would wake up before daylight to pray in the snow, in icy coldness and in the rain.' He lived his life like this for six years until he finally escaped back to his family in Wales. He was so happy when he got back to his family that he praised God for answering his prayers.

Child holds up the cross/crucifix and places it in the sacred space

Reader 4: When he grew older, St Patrick decided that he wanted to become a priest. After some years, he was made a bishop. Many years later St Patrick had a dream. In that dream the people of Ireland were calling him to come back. St Patrick decided that he would return to the people of Ireland, to tell them about Jesus.

Child holds up the picture of a bishop's crozier and places it in the sacred space

Reader 5: St Patrick returned to Ireland in about 432 AD. He built his first church in a place called Saul in County Down and spent the next thirty years going around Ireland telling people about Christianity. He is most famously known for using the shamrock that was growing wild in the countryside, to explain the Holy Trinity – three persons, in one God. St Patrick died around 461 AD. His grave is in Downpatrick.

Child holds up the picture of shamrock and places it in the sacred space

If you have a traditional group of musicians in the school they may wish to play at this time

Leader: As we gather here today to remember St Patrick, we do so in thanksgiving for the gift of faith which he brought to this land. The response to each prayer is, 'Glory to God forever'.

All: Glory to God forever.

Reader 6: We pray for all who strive to bring the message of Christianity to different parts of the world. *(Response)*

Reader 7: We pray for all who are preparing to be baptised at this time. *(Response)*

Reader 8: We pray for all who have been unjustly imprisoned. *(Response)*

Reader 9: We pray for all Irish people across the world. *(Response)*

Leader: We bring all of our prayers together in our Prayer to Jesus/*Paidir d'Íosa*. This prayer is based on a prayer that was written by St Patrick himself.

All: Christ be with me .../*Críost liom ...*

Leader: We finish with an old Irish blessing. The response at the end of each line is 'Amen'.

May the Lord bless you and keep you. *(Response)*

May his face shine on you and be gracious to you. *(Response)*

May he look upon you with kindness and give you his peace. *(Response)*

Leader: And may God bless us all. In the name of the Father, and of the Son and of the Holy Spirit.

All: Amen.

Leader: In the name of the Father, and of the Son and of the Holy Spirit.

All: Amen.

Closing Hymn: ♪ *Alleluia* (Track 3)

9. St Patrick

389 AD

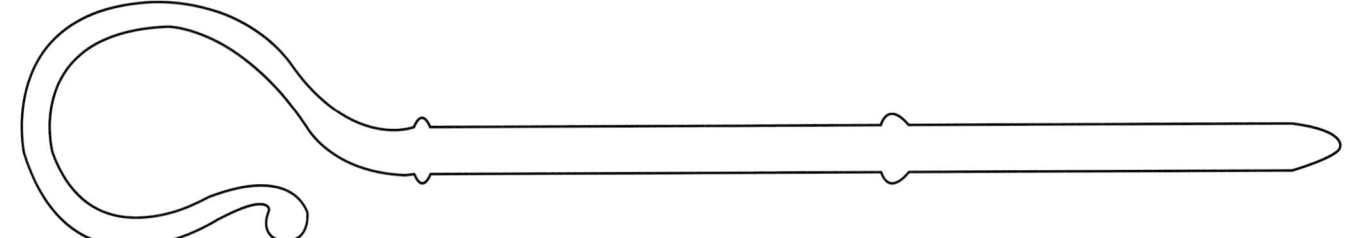

Term 2

10. St Joseph

For the Leader: The Feast of St Joseph is celebrated on March 19. St Joseph was Mary's husband and Jesus' foster father. He is the patron saint of fathers, workers and carpenters, and is protector of the Universal Church. During this prayer assembly, we encourage children to pray for their fathers, grandfathers, godfathers, or whoever helps to mind them like Joseph helped Mary to mind Jesus. You may need to be sensitive to any children who have been bereaved or separated from the men who care for them.

> **You will need:**
> - Four children to read
>
> **Sacred Space:**
> - White cloth
> - Bible
> - Candle
> - Cross/Crucifix
> - An image of St Joseph, or his figure from the Christmas crib
> - Some tools, representing St Joseph's trade as a carpenter

Opening Song: ♪ *They Care For Me* (Track 29)

Leader: In the name of the Father, and of the Son and of the Holy Spirit.

All: Amen.

Leader: Let us begin with a prayer to our Guardian Angel:

All: Angel sent by God to guide me,
be my light and walk beside me;
be my guardian and protect me;
on the paths of life direct me.
Amen.

Leader: We gather together today on the Feast of St Joseph. St Joseph was Mary's husband. He helped her to take care of Jesus. We also remember and pray for our fathers/daddies, our grandfathers/granddads, our godfathers, or anyone else who helps to take care of us. Let us begin by listening to some stories about Joseph. This will help us to see how he was a good foster father to Jesus.

Reader 1: When Joseph found out that Mary was going to have a baby, he was very worried and upset. He even planned to break off their engagement. However, an angel appeared to Joseph in a dream, and told him not to be afraid to marry Mary. Joseph trusted the angel's message, and he and Mary got married.

Leader: What does this story tell us about Joseph? (*Invite children to think in silence or to answer aloud, whichever is most appropriate*)
We can learn a lot from the way Joseph trusted in God's plan for him and Mary. We pray that we can be trusting too.

Reader 2: Around the time that Mary was due to give birth to Jesus, the Roman emperor Caesar Augustus ordered a census. So, everyone had to travel to the place where their family was from. Joseph was a descendent of King David, so he and Mary had to travel to Bethlehem. While they were there, the time came for Mary to have the baby, but because there were so many people in Bethlehem, there was no room for them to stay in an inn. Mary and Joseph eventually found a stable, and it was there that Jesus was born.

Leader: What does this story tell us about Joseph? (*Invite children to think in silence or to answer aloud, whichever is most appropriate*)
We can learn a lot from the way Joseph didn't give up and kept looking for somewhere for his family to stay. We pray that we will always keep trying, just like Joseph.

Reader 3: Soon after Jesus was born, Joseph had another dream. In this dream, an angel told him to take Mary and Jesus to Egypt, because they were not safe in Bethlehem. Again, Joseph did as the angel said, and the Holy Family was kept safe.

Leader: What does this story tell us about Joseph?
(*Invite children to think in silence or to answer aloud, whichever is most appropriate*)
We can learn a lot from the way Joseph did what God asked him to do. We pray that we will always be able to do what God wants us to do, even if it is hard.

Reader 4: When Jesus was twelve years old, Mary and Joseph went to Jerusalem with their family and friends for the Passover festival. When the celebrations were over, Mary and Joseph left, but Jesus had stayed in the city without telling them. When they could not find him, Mary and Joseph became very worried. They immediately went back to Jerusalem and started looking for him there. After three days, they eventually found Jesus, sitting in the temple.

Leader: What does this story tell us about Joseph?
(*Invite children to think in silence or to answer aloud, whichever is most appropriate*)
We can tell that Joseph loved Jesus very much because he was very worried about him when he couldn't find him. We pray that we will always show love to our families, especially when they are in need.

So, we know that St Joseph was a trusting, loving man, who listened to God and who didn't give up easily. Many of us know people who are just like St Joseph. It may be our fathers/daddies, grandfathers/granddads, godfathers, or someone else who helps to take care of us. Let us take a moment to think about one of these people in particular, and to ask St Joseph to bless them in a special way today.

♪ *Play Reflective Music* (Track 22)

Close your eyes for a moment. Think about the person you want to pray for. Try to see their picture in your head. Think about what makes them like St Joseph. Think about a time when they showed you that they love you, or a time when they took care of you. (*Pause*)

Using your inside voice that no-one else can hear, say 'Thank You' to God for this person. Ask God to bless them. Ask St Joseph to pray for them. (*Pause*)

When you are ready, you can open your eyes.

We know that Jesus prayed constantly to his Father in heaven. He asked us to pray to God the Father too. And so, as Jesus asked us, we dare to say:

All: Our Father .../Ár nAthair ...

Leader: Let us pray:

Loving God,
We thank you for the example set for us by St Joseph. Bless our fathers/daddies, grandfathers/granddads, godfathers, and all those who help to take care of us. May we also act like St Joseph, by showing our love for you and for our families.
We make this prayer through Christ our Lord.

All: Amen.

Leader: In the name of the Father, and of the Son and of the Holy Spirit.

All: Amen.

Closing Hymn: ♪ *The Lord's Prayer* (Track 27)

Term 2

11. Lenten Penitential Service (For Senior Classes)

For the Leader: Lent is a time of prayer, fasting and almsgiving in preparation for the joyful season of Easter. As part of our preparations, we are also encouraged to celebrate the Sacrament of Reconciliation. In fact, many of the children in our schools may celebrate the sacrament for the first time during the Lenten season. It may be possible to invite a priest from the parish to celebrate the sacrament with the children during this Lenten Penitential Service. Alternatively, you can use this prayer assembly as a time for those gathered to reflect on their lives, and then encourage them to celebrate the Sacrament of Reconciliation in the parish church. It would be helpful to let them know the days and times when the sacrament is celebrated locally.

> **You will need:**
> - Six children to read
>
> **Sacred Space:**
> - Violet cloth
> - Bible, open at Luke 19:1-10
> - Candle
> - Cross/Crucifix
> - A wilderness space containing some sand, twigs and stones

Opening Song: ♪ *Song Of Repentance* (Track 24)

Leader: In the name of the Father, and of the Son and of the Holy Spirit.

All: Amen.

Leader: Let us begin with a prayer to our Guardian Angel:

All: Angel sent by God to guide me,
be my light and walk beside me;
be my guardian and protect me;
on the paths of life direct me. Amen.

Leader: At the beginning of Lent, ashes were placed on our foreheads and we were invited to 'Turn away from sin and be faithful to the Gospel'. We gather together today to reflect on our lives, and to think about those times when we could have made better choices as followers of Jesus. Together, let us admit that there have been times when we were not faithful to the Gospel message:

All: I confess to almighty God
and to you, my brothers and sisters,
that I have greatly sinned
in my thoughts and in my words,
in what I have done
and in what I have failed to do,
through my fault, through my fault,
through my most grievous fault;
therefore I ask blessed Mary ever-Virgin,
all the Angels and Saints,
and you, my brothers and sisters,
to pray for me to the Lord our God.

Leader: May almighty God have mercy on us, forgive us our sins, and bring us to everlasting life.

All: Amen.

Leader: Through his words and actions, Jesus showed us the importance of forgiveness. Let us listen to the story of Jesus' encounter with a man named Zacchaeus. It is a reading from the Holy Gospel according to Luke (19:1-10):

Reader 1: Jesus was going through Jericho, where a man named Zacchaeus lived. He was in charge of collecting taxes and was very rich. Jesus was heading his way, and Zacchaeus wanted to see what he was like. But Zacchaeus was a short man and could not see over the crowd. So he ran ahead and climbed up into a sycamore tree. When Jesus got there, he looked up and said, 'Zacchaeus, hurry down! I want to stay with you today.' Zacchaeus hurried down and gladly welcomed Jesus. Everyone who saw this started grumbling, 'This man Zacchaeus is a sinner!

And Jesus is going home to eat with him.' Later that day Zacchaeus stood up and said to the Lord, 'I will give half of my property to the poor. And I will now pay back four times as much to everyone I have ever cheated.' Jesus said to Zacchaeus, 'Today you and your family have been saved, because you are a true son of Abraham. The Son of Man came to look for and to save people who are lost.'

The Gospel of the Lord.

All: Praise to you, Lord Jesus Christ.

Leader: With Jesus' help, Zacchaeus realised that he was not living his life in the right way. He decided to try to make up for what he had done wrong by paying back the people he had cheated and even giving them more than he had taken. Jesus was happy that Zacchaeus had made this choice. Jesus is just as happy when we realise that we have done something wrong, and we choose to say sorry. Let's take a moment to think about those things for which we would like to say sorry. The response to each prayer is 'Jesus, forgive us'.

All: Jesus, forgive us.

Reader 2: It is important to make time for God in our lives. If we have forgotten to pray, or if we haven't managed to go to Mass every week, Jesus, forgive us. (*Response*)

Reader 3: Jesus told his disciples to love one another just as he had loved them. If we have not shown love to our brothers, sisters or friends, Jesus, forgive us. (*Response*)

Reader 4: We should always respect other people's property. If we have borrowed things without returning them, or taken something that does not belong to us, Jesus, forgive us. (*Response*)

Reader 5: Jesus cared for those who were sick, poor or left out. If we have not reached out to those who need our help, Jesus, forgive us. (*Response*)

Reader 6: Jesus obeyed his mother, Mary. If we have not done as our family, teachers and helpers asked us to, Jesus, forgive us. (*Response*)

If the Sacrament of Reconciliation is being celebrated as part of this assembly, now is the time for individual Confession and Absolution. If the Sacrament of Reconciliation is not being celebrated as part of this prayer assembly, continue below.

Leader: Together, let us say the Act of Sorrow, as a sign that we want to turn back to God:

All: O my God,
I thank you for loving me,
I am sorry for all my sins,
for not loving others and not loving you.
Help me to live like Jesus and not sin again.
Amen.

Leader: As part of the Our Father, we pray that 'we forgive those who trespass against us'. As a sign that we can do just that, let us offer each other a sign of peace.

Children offer a sign of peace to those next to them.

Leader: Let us pray:

Loving God,
We thank you for sending us your son, Jesus, to show us how to live.
Give us the strength to continue with our Lenten promises during this special season,
so that we may more joyfully share in the celebration of the Resurrection.
We make this prayer through Christ our Lord.

All: Amen.

Leader: In the name of the Father, and of the Son and of the Holy Spirit.

All: Amen.

Closing Hymn: ♪ *Wilderness* (Track 35)

Term 2

12. Holy Week

For the Leader: As schools are on holidays during Holy Week, you may like to use this prayer assembly on the week before the Easter holidays. It focuses on the key moments of Jesus' Passion, Death and Resurrection:

- Palm Sunday: Jesus arrives in Jerusalem
- Holy Thursday: Jesus shares the Last Supper with his disciples
- Good Friday: Jesus dies on the cross
- Holy Saturday: Jesus lays in the tomb
- Easter Sunday: God raises Jesus to new life

> **You will need:**
> - Five children to read
> - Seven children to carry symbols to the sacred space
>
> **Sacred Space:**
> - Red or white cloth (both colours are used during Holy Week)
> - Bible, open at Mark 16:1-8
> - Cross/Crucifix
> - Other items will be added to the sacred space during the service: a palm branch, a bowl of water, bread, a hammer, a stone, a candle

Opening Song: ♪ *Quiet And Still* (Track 21)

Leader: In the name of the Father, and of the Son and of the Holy Spirit.

All: Amen.

Leader: Let us begin with a prayer to our Guardian Angel:

All: Angel sent by God to guide me,
be my light and walk beside me;
be my guardian and protect me;
on the paths of life direct me.
Amen.

Leader: We gather together today as our Lenten journey comes to a close. Soon, Holy Week will begin. During Holy Week, we remember how Jesus died, and what he did in the days leading up to his death. Holy Week begins on Palm Sunday and ends on Holy Saturday night. Let us listen to the story of these important days.

Reader 1: It is Palm Sunday. Jesus begins his journey to Jerusalem, where he plans to eat the Passover meal with his friends. When they are near the city, two of his disciples bring him a donkey. Jesus rides the donkey into Jerusalem. As they approached the city, people come and lay palms on the ground. With great joy, they sing 'Blessed is he who comes in the name of the Lord'. They are excited to see Jesus. However, there are other who are not happy with Jesus. They tell him to stop the people saying such things about him. But Jesus does not stop them. The people praise God and lay palms on the ground as Jesus enters the city.

♪ *Play verse one of 'Imagine You Were There' (Track 17). As the song is playing, one child holds up a palm branch and places it in the sacred space.*

Reader 2: It is Holy Thursday. Jesus and his friends share the Passover meal. As they gather, Jesus washes the feet of his disciples. The disciples do not feel comfortable with this, but Jesus insists. He says that they must do the same for others. After that, they eat. During the meal, Jesus takes bread, says the blessing and gives it to them, telling them that it is his Body. At the end of the meal, he takes the cup filled with wine and says the blessing over it. He tells them that it is his Blood. Jesus tells the disciples to do this again, in his memory, so that he can always be with them.

♪ *Play verse two of 'Imagine You Were There' (Track 17). As the song is playing, one child holds up a bowl of water and places it in the sacred space, and a second child holds up some bread and places that in the sacred space too.*

Reader 3: It is Good Friday. Jesus has been arrested by armed guards. He is beaten and stripped of his clothes. A crown of thorns is put on his head. He is mocked and denied by his friends. The people are asked if they want him to live or to die. The say 'Crucify him!' He is made to carry a cross out of the city onto a high hill. There, he is nailed to the cross and his dies. His mother Mary is with him.

♪ *Play verse three of 'Imagine You Were There' (Track 17). As the song is playing, one child holds up a hammer and places it in the sacred space.*

Reader 4: It is Holy Saturday. After his death on Good Friday, Jesus is taken from the cross and is laid in a tomb. He remains there all day Saturday.

♪ *Play verse four of 'Imagine You Were There' (Track 17). As the song is playing, one child holds up a stone and places it in the sacred space.*

Leader: That is the story of Jesus' suffering and death during Holy Week. Jesus was killed unfairly by people who did not understand his message of love. That is not the end of the story, however, because on Easter Sunday morning the most amazing thing happened. Let's listen to the story.

Reader 5: *A reading from the Holy Gospel according to Mark (16:1-8)*
After the Sabbath, Mary Magdalene, Salome, and Mary the mother of James bought some spices to put on Jesus' body. Very early on Sunday morning, just as the sun was coming up, they went to the tomb. On their way, they were asking one another, 'Who will roll the stone away from the entrance for us?' But when they looked, they saw that the stone had already been rolled away. And it was a huge stone!

The women went into the tomb, and on the right side they saw a young man in a white robe sitting there. They were alarmed. The man said, 'Don't be alarmed! You are looking for Jesus from Nazareth, who was nailed to a cross. God has raised him to life, and he isn't here. You can see the place where they put his body. Now go and tell his disciples, and especially Peter, that he will go ahead of you to Galilee. You will see him there, just as he told you.'

The Gospel of the Lord.

All: Praise to you, Lord Jesus Christ.

♪ *Play verse five of 'Imagine You Were There' (Track 17). As the song is playing, one child holds up the candle and places it in the sacred space, where it is lit.*

Leader: Jesus, our friend,
As we remember the story of your suffering and death during this Holy Week,
we pray for those who are still suffering unjustly in the world.
We pray that their pain will one day be lifted.
Help us to make the journey with you through this Holy Week, from suffering and death to new life.
We make this prayer through Christ our Lord.

All: Amen.

Leader: In the name of the Father, and of the Son and of the Holy Spirit.

All: Amen.

Closing Hymn: ♪ *Alleluia* (Track 3)

Term 3

1. Easter Season

For the Leader: We can sometimes think of, and indeed celebrate, Easter as a one-day event. However, the Easter season lasts for a fifty-day period, which culminates in the Feast of Pentecost. This prayer service offers your school community an opportunity to celebrate the Easter season even though Easter Sunday has passed. You can retain the Easter character of your school's sacred space throughout the Easter season as a visual reminder of the Resurrection.

> **You will need:**
> - Six children to read
> - Child(ren) to hold the bowls of holy water at the exit points of the assembly area
>   or
> - A leafy twig, if you wish to sprinkle holy water
>
> **Sacred Space:**
> - White cloth
> - Bible, open at Matthew 27:57-60, and Mark 16:1-7
> - Candle
> - Cross/Crucifix. If possible, place a white cloth over the arms of cross, reminiscent of the shroud left in the tomb
> - A poster on which is written the word 'Alleluia'. An example is given on page 77. You may like to ask children to colour it in before the service begins
> - Some Easter lilies or other flowers, symbolising new growth
> - Some eggs, which symbolise new birth
> - Some holy water in a bowl (or two, depending on the size of your school). Children will be invited to bless themselves with this water at the end of the prayer service. Alternatively you can sprinkle the holy water using the leafy twig

Opening Song: ♪ *This Is The Day* (Track 30)

Leader: In the name of the Father, and of the Son and of the Holy Spirit.

All: Amen.

Leader: Let us begin with our Prayer to the Holy Spirit, which we will say at all our prayer assemblies this term:

All: Holy Spirit, I want to do what is right. Help me.
Holy Spirit, I want to live like Jesus. Guide me.
Holy Spirit, I want to pray like Jesus. Teach me. Amen.

Leader: We gather together today to celebrate Jesus' resurrection. Jesus died a cruel and horrible death, and his friends were upset and scared. However, God raised Jesus to new life as a sign for them, and for all of us, that goodness will always win over sin and evil. Let us remind ourselves of what happened. We will begin on Good Friday, when Jesus died on the cross.

Reader 1: *A reading from the Holy Gospel according to Matthew (27:57-60)*
That evening a rich disciple named Joseph went and asked for Jesus' body. Pilate gave orders for it to be given to Joseph, who took the body and wrapped it in a clean linen cloth. Then Joseph put the body in his own tomb that had been cut into solid rock and had never been used. He rolled a big stone against the entrance to the tomb and went away.

The Gospel of the Lord.

All: Praise to you, Lord Jesus Christ.

Leader: Image how Joseph and Jesus' other friends must have felt that evening. What words would you use to describe them? (*Invite children to think in silence or to answer aloud, whichever is most appropriate*)

Scared, sad and afraid, Jesus' friends left the tomb. Three days later, on Easter Sunday morning, some of them returned. Let us listen to the story of what happened that day.

Reader 2: *A reading from the Holy Gospel according to Mark (16:1-7)*

After the Sabbath, Mary Magdalene, Salome, and Mary the mother of James bought some spices to put on Jesus' body. Very early on Sunday morning, just as the sun was coming up, they went to the tomb. On their way, they were asking one another, 'Who will roll the stone away from the entrance for us?' But when they looked, they saw that the stone had already been rolled away. And it was a huge stone! The women went into the tomb, and on the right side they saw a young man in a white robe sitting there. They were alarmed. The man said, 'Don't be alarmed! You are looking for Jesus from Nazareth, who was nailed to a cross. God has raised him to life, and he isn't here. You can see the place where they put his body. Now go and tell his disciples.'

The Gospel of the Lord.

All: Praise to you, Lord Jesus Christ.

Leader: How do you think the women felt this time? *(Invite children to think in silence or to answer aloud, whichever is most appropriate)*

At this time every year, we celebrate, because we too are happy that God raised Jesus to new life. Sometimes, when we are happy, we might sing or cheer; for example, we could say 'Hip Hip Hurray!' We can show we are happy that Jesus is risen by saying or singing 'Alleluia'. Let us offer our prayers of thanksgiving to God. The response to each prayer is, 'Alleluia! Amen'.

All: Alleluia! Amen.

Reader 3: Thank you, God, for giving us your Son, Jesus, to show us how to live and how to love. We pray to the Lord. *(Response)*

Reader 4: Thank you, God, for giving us families who care for us, and who show us your love. We pray to the Lord. *(Response)*

Reader 5: Thank you, God, for giving us friends to play with and a school in which to learn and grow. We pray to the Lord. *(Response)*

Reader 6: Thank you, God, for giving us the gift of your beautiful world. We pray to the Lord. *(Response)*

Leader: Every Easter Saturday, on the night when we celebrate Jesus' Resurrection, the priest blesses some holy water. We call this holy water 'Easter water'. Water gives life to all things, and helps all things to grow. God also gives life, and helps all things to grow. As we leave this place today, we will use holy water as a reminder that we are happy to live and grow in friendship with Jesus.

Invite the child(ren) you have selected to stand at the exits of the prayer space with the bowls containing holy water. Alternatively, you can use a leafy twig to sprinkle the holy water on those gathered.

Leader: Let us pray:

Loving God,
We thank you for raising your Son Jesus, from the dead. Help us to spread the Good News of his Resurrection with those we meet during this Easter season.
We pray that we will be kind and helpful, so that everyone will know that we are your followers.
We make this prayer through Christ our Lord.

All: Amen.

Leader: In the name of the Father, and of the Son and of the Holy Spirit.

All: Amen.

Closing Hymn: ♪ *Alleluia* (Track 3)

1. Easter Season

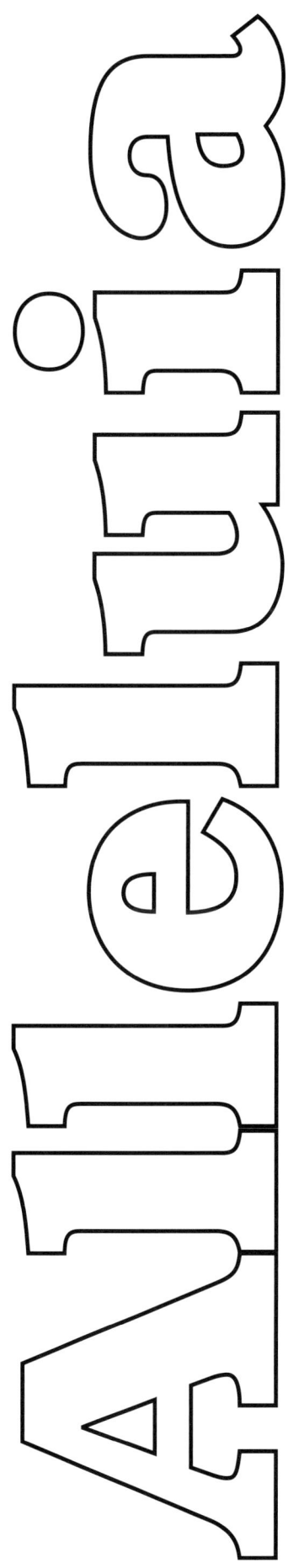

Term 3

2. Mary

For the Leader: May is the month that is traditionally associated with devotion to Mary, the Mother of God. By honouring Mary, we are also honouring God, who bestowed on her the great privilege of being mother of Jesus. Traditionally, children create altars in honour of Mary in their homes and classrooms during the month of May. Some schools and parishes also organise a May procession.

You will need:
- Two children to read
- One child to lead a decade of the Rosary
- Some children to carry flowers to the sacred space

Sacred Space:
- White or blue cloth
- Bible, open at Luke 2:41-51
- Candle
- Cross/Crucifix
- Statue or image of Mary
- Some flowers
- Rosary beads

Opening Song: ♪ *Mary, Our Mother* (Track 20)

Leader: In the name of the Father, and of the Son and of the Holy Spirit.

All: Amen.

Leader: Let us begin with our Prayer to the Holy Spirit:

All: Holy Spirit, I want to do what is right. Help me.
Holy Spirit, I want to live like Jesus. Guide me.
Holy Spirit, I want to pray like Jesus. Teach me. Amen.

Leader: We gather together today to celebrate May as the month of Mary. When the angel Gabriel came to Mary and asked her to be the mother of Jesus, she said that she was happy to do what God wanted. She and Joseph cared for Jesus while he was growing up, and helped him to become the person God wanted him to be. Let us listen to one story about Jesus, Mary and Joseph.

Reader 1: *A reading from the Holy Gospel according to Luke (2:41-51)*
Every year Jesus' parents went to Jerusalem for Passover. And when Jesus was twelve years old, they all went there as usual for the celebration. After Passover his parents left, but they did not know that Jesus had stayed on in the city. They thought he was travelling with some other people, and they went a whole day before they started looking for him. When they could not find him with their relatives and friends, they went back to Jerusalem and started looking for him there. Three days later they found Jesus sitting in the temple, listening to the teachers and asking them questions. Everyone who heard him was surprised at how much he knew and at the answers he gave. When his parents found him, they were amazed. His mother said, 'Son, why have you done this to us? Your father and I have been very worried, and we have been searching for you!' Jesus answered, 'Why did you have to look for me? Didn't you know that I would be in my Father's house?' But they did not understand what he meant. Jesus went back to Nazareth with his parents and obeyed them. His mother kept on thinking about all that had happened.

The Gospel of the Lord.

All: Praise to you, Lord Jesus Christ.

♪ *Play Reflective Music* (Track 22). *As the music is playing, invite a child/some children to place flowers in the sacred space.*

Leader: The Rosary is a special prayer. In it, we remember key moments in the life of Jesus. It is also a prayer that honours Mary. We will now pray one decade of the Rosary in honour of Mary. We will pray the fifth Joyful Mystery, The Finding in the Temple.

Invite one student to come forward to lead one decade of the Rosary. A decade of the Rosary is composed of one Our Father, ten Hail Marys and one Glory be to the Father. The student who is leading the Rosary prays the first half of each prayer, and the rest of the group respond with the second half.

Leader: Mary is known by many different names. Let us use some of these now. The response to each prayer is, 'Pray for us'.

All: Pray for us.

Reader 2: Holy Mary (*Response*)
Mother or God. (*Response*)
Mother most pure. (*Response*)
Mother most faithful. (*Response*)
Mother most merciful. (*Response*)
Queen of angels. (*Response*)
Queen of all saints. (*Response*)
Queen of apostles. (*Response*)
Queen of peace. (*Response*)
Queen of Ireland. (*Response*)

Leader: Let us pray:

Loving God,
We thank you for the example of Mary, whom you chose from among all women to be the mother of your Son.
May she watch over us in our lives as she watched over and cared for Jesus.
Help us to always have the courage to say 'Yes' to what you ask of us, just as she did.
We make this prayer through Christ our Lord.

All: Amen.

Leader: In the name of the Father, and of the Son and of the Holy Spirit.

All: Amen.

Closing Hymn: ♪ *Magnificat* (Track 19)

Term 3

3. St Columba (St Columcille)

For the Leader: The Feast of St Columba, who is also known as St Columcille, is celebrated on June 9. Together with Brigid and Patrick, Columba is one of Ireland's three patron saints. Like many monks of his time, St Columba travelled widely, preaching the Gospel. He eventually travelled as far as Iona, an island off the coast of Scotland, where he established a monastery. It was there that the Book of Kells was produced. This prayer assembly focuses on the missionary aspect of St Columba's life, and encourages all in the school community to be inspired by his example.

> **You will need:**
> - Eight children to read
>
> **Sacred Space:**
> - Green cloth
> - Bible
> - Candle
> - Cross/Crucifix
> - Celtic designs or reproductions from the Book of Kells

Opening Song: ♪ *Christ Be Beside Me* (Track 6)

Leader: In the name of the Father, and of the Son and of the Holy Spirit.

All: Amen.

Leader: Let us begin with our Prayer to the Holy Spirit:

All: Holy Spirit, I want to do what is right. Help me.
Holy Spirit, I want to live like Jesus. Guide me.
Holy Spirit, I want to pray like Jesus. Teach me. Amen.

Leader: We gather together today on the Feast of St Columba. St Columba lived about one hundred years after St Brigid. He was born in County Dongeal, but he travelled all over Ireland and even abroad. Let us learn some more about his life:

Reader 1: It is believed that Columba belonged to a royal family and so he was destined to become a prince and then a king. However, while he was still very young, Columba was sent to live with a priest called Finian. The more time he spent with Finian, learning about Jesus' message of love, the more Columba knew that the princely life was not for him. He decided to become a monk, and then a priest, and to dedicate his life to God.

Reader 2: Columba wanted other men to join him, so that they could live together as a community, doing God's work. So, he founded a monastery in County Derry, and a second one in County Laois. Many men came to live at the monastery, and they spent their time praying, studying the Bible, and working outdoors. Columba spent a lot of time travelling around Ireland, teaching people about Jesus and trying to help them to live the way God wants.

Reader 3: Columba knew that there were people outside of Ireland who had never heard about Jesus, and he wanted to teach them. So, he left Ireland for an island called Iona, which is just off the coast of Scotland, and set up another monastery there. Lots of people travelled to Iona to hear Columba preach God's message of love, and many stayed there with him. Columba was the first Irish monk to spread the Gospel message to people in other countries. In the years since his death, many hundreds and thousands of people have followed his example.

Leader: St Columba knew how important it is to spread God's message of love. We here at _____ school know that we have to do the same. However, we don't have to travel to other countries or even all around Ireland. We can bring God's love to the world right here, by helping others, by sharing what we have with people who need it, and by being kind to each other. We can also show our love for God by praying to him, so let us do that now. The response to each prayer is, 'St Columba, pray for us.'

All: St Columba, pray for us.

Reader 4: St Columba lived a life of prayer. May we too take time to listen to God, so that we will be guided by his word. (*Response*)

Reader 5: St Columba was inspired by his teacher. May we always be open to learning from others. (*Response*)

Reader 6: St Columba gave up his wealth to live a life devoted to God. May we too be generous with what we have. (*Response*)

Reader 7: St Columba brought the Good News of God's love to others. May we too share that same message of love with the people we meet. (*Response*)

Reader 8: We pray for those who follow in the footsteps of St Columba by leaving their homes and their families to spread the Word of God. (*Response*)

Leader: Together, let us give glory to God, just as St Columba did:

All: Glory be to the Father .../*Glóir don Athair ...*

Leader: Let us pray:

Loving God,
We thank you for the life of Columba, who gave up everything to follow the message of Jesus.
Bless all those who continue in this mission today.
Help us to play our part in spreading the Good News of your love in our home, school and parish communities.
We make this prayer through Christ our Lord.

All: Amen.

Leader: In the name of the Father, and of the Son and of the Holy Spirit.

All: Amen.

Closing Hymn: ♪ *Go Tell Everyone* (Track 15)

3. St Columba (St Columcille)

Term 3

4. The Ascension

For the Leader: The Solemnity of the Ascension is traditionally celebrated forty days after Easter Sunday, which means that it falls on a Thursday. However, the Catholic Church in Ireland celebrates this feast day on the following Sunday, exactly six weeks after Easter Sunday. The Feast of the Ascension marks the final appearance of Jesus after his Resurrection. It is at this time that he instructs the Apostles to 'Go and preach the Good News to everyone in the world' (Mark 16:15). After that, he ascended into heaven. World Communications Day coincides with the Feast of the Ascension. On World Communications Day we think about how we communicate God's message in the world today.

> **You will need:**
> - Four children to read
> - Four children to perform actions
> - A poster on which is written the text message 'God lvs u!', which is on page 85
>
> **Sacred Space:**
> - White cloth
> - Bible, open at Acts of the Apostles 1:7-11
> - Candle
> - Cross/Crucifix

Opening Song: ♪ *Go Tell Everyone* (Track 15)

Leader: In the name of the Father, and of the Son and of the Holy Spirit.

All: Amen.

Leader: Let us begin with our Prayer to the Holy Spirit:

All: Holy Spirit, I want to do what is right. Help me.
Holy Spirit, I want to live like Jesus. Guide me.
Holy Spirit, I want to pray like Jesus. Teach me. Amen.

Leader: We gather together today to reflect on the Feast of the Ascension. Can you guess how many days it has been since we celebrated Jesus' Resurrection on Easter Sunday? (*Invite children to think in silence or to answer aloud, whichever is most appropriate*)

It has, in fact, been forty days since Easter Sunday. And in these forty days, Jesus appeared many times to his disciples. He helped them to understand his life and his message. But Jesus could not stay with his Apostles forever. He belongs with God the Father in heaven. So, let's listen to what happened on Ascension Day, forty days after he was raised from the dead.

Reader 1: *A reading from the Acts of the Apostles (1:7-11)*
Jesus said to them ' ... the Holy Spirit will come upon you and give you power. Then you will tell everyone about me in Jerusalem, in all Judea, in Samaria, and everywhere in the world.' After Jesus had said this and while they were watching, he was taken up into a cloud. They could not see him, but as he went up, they kept looking up into the sky. Suddenly two men dressed in white clothes were standing there beside them. They said, 'Why are you men from Galilee standing here and looking up into the sky? Jesus has been taken to heaven. But he will come back in the same way that you have seen him go.'

The Word of the Lord.

All: Thanks be to God.

Leader: Now before Jesus ascended into heaven, he told the disciples to do something. Who can remember what that was? (*Invite children to think in silence or to answer aloud, whichever is most appropriate*)

Jesus told them to tell everyone in the whole world about him. And that is exactly what they did. Can you believe that? Back then, there were only a few people in the world who even knew Jesus' name. Today, more than two billion people are followers of Jesus! Do you think Jesus' friends did a good job?

The thing is, the job is not yet done. Jesus' followers still have to tell people about Jesus, and show everyone that they are his friends. And that doesn't just mean other people – it means us! So, how can we communicate Jesus' message in our home, school and parish communities? Let's think about it.

Reader 2: We can share the Good News by the way we treat others.

Two children wave and smile at each other

Reader 3: We can send text messages that share the Good News.

Child holds up the poster from page 85 and places it in the sacred space.

Reader 4: We can use signs and actions to share the Good News.

Child signs 'Jesus loves you', as follows:

Jesus – child points to the centre of each hand, indicating where the nails were placed
Loves – child embraces themselves in a hug
You – child points to another person with their index figure outstretched

Leader: Take a moment to choose one thing that you can do today to share the Good News of Jesus with others. (*Pause*)

Let us pray:

Loving God,
We thank you for the gift of your Son, Jesus, who shared the Good News with us.
Today, as we remember his Ascension, we pray for all who have not yet heard the Good News of your love.
Give us the courage to share your message in all that we say and all that we do.
We make this prayer through Christ our Lord.

All: Amen.

Leader: In the name of the Father, and of the Son and of the Holy Spirit.

All: Amen.

Closing Hymn: ♪ *Go Now In Peace* (Track 14)

4. The Ascension

God lvs u!

Term 3

5. Pentecost

For the Leader: Pentecost Sunday marks the end of the Easter season, fifty days after Easter Sunday. It celebrates the outpouring of God's Holy Spirit on the apostles, and the beginning (or 'birth-day') of the Church. It was on this day that the Apostles, once fearful and afraid to even be seen in public, went out onto the streets of Jerusalem to tell the people the story of Jesus Christ. As Christians we believe that they were enabled to do this by the power of God's Spirit. Today, the same Spirit is given to us for the first time in the Sacrament of Baptism. We receive the fullness of the gift of the Holy Spirit in the Sacrament of Confirmation. For this reason, you may like to involve those children who have been confirmed during the academic year in this prayer assembly.

> **You will need:**
> - Eight children to read
>
> **Sacred Space:**
> - Red cloth
> - Bible, open at Acts 2:1-4
> - Candle
> - Cross/Crucifix

Opening Song: ♪ *Spirit Anthem* (Track 25)

Leader: In the name of the Father, and of the Son and of the Holy Spirit.

All: Amen.

Leader: Let us begin with our Prayer to the Holy Spirit:

All: Holy Spirit, I want to do what is right. Help me.
Holy Spirit, I want to live like Jesus. Guide me.
Holy Spirit, I want to pray like Jesus. Teach me. Amen.

Leader: We gather together today to celebrate the Feast of Pentecost. On Pentecost Sunday, we remember that, even though Jesus went back to heaven after his Resurrection, he did not leave his friends and followers alone. He knew that they would need help in order to spread the Good News of God's love. So, he sent them the gift of God's Holy Spirit to be their helper and their guide in all that they had to do. Let us listen to the story of what happened on that day:

Reader 1: *A reading from the Acts of the Apostles (2:1-4)*
On the day of Pentecost all the Lord's followers were together in one place. Suddenly there was a noise from heaven like the sound of a mighty wind! It filled the house where they were meeting. Then they saw what looked like fiery tongues moving in all directions, and a tongue came and settled on each person there. The Holy Spirit took control of everyone, and they began speaking whatever languages the Spirit let them speak.

The Word of the Lord.

All: Thanks be to God.

Leader: The Spirit of God gave the Apostles the gifts they needed to spread the Good News brought by Jesus. These same gifts are given to all of us on the day that we are baptised, and they are strengthened in us on the day we celebrate our Confirmation. Let us hear about the gifts that God gives to each of us, by the power of the Holy Spirit:

Reader 2: The Spirit gives us the gift of Wisdom, so that we can know the right thing to do and the right way to treat others.

Reader 3: The Spirit gives us the gift of Understanding, so that we can recognise how other people feel, and so that we can treat them as we should.

Reader 4: The Spirit gives us the gift of Right Judgement, so that we can make good decisions that will make the world a better place.

Reader 5: The Spirit gives us the gift of Courage, so that we are not afraid to stand up for what we believe in, even when it is not the popular thing to do.

Reader 6: The Spirit gives us the gift of Knowledge, so that we can learn more about God and how to live our lives as followers of Jesus.

Reader 7: The Spirit gives us the gift of Reverence, so that we can respect God, others and the world around us.

Reader 8: The Spirit gives us the gift of Wonder and Awe in God's Presence, so that we can recognise and appreciate how wonderful the world is, and how wonderful God is.

Leader: Together, let us pray to the Holy Spirit, asking that these gifts be strengthened in us so that we, like the Apostles, may be able to live the best lives we can as friends of Jesus. The response to each prayer is, 'Come, Holy Spirit'.

All: Come, Holy Spirit.

Reader 2: Come, Holy Spirit, when we need to work out the right thing to do. *(Response)*

Reader 3: Come, Holy Spirit, when we need to see things from other people's point of view. *(Response)*

Reader 4: Come, Holy Spirit, when we have a difficult decision to make. *(Response)*

Reader 5: Come, Holy Spirit, when we find it hard to stand up for what we believe in. *(Response)*

Reader 6: Come, Holy Spirit, when we want to learn more about God, so that we can live as followers of Jesus. *(Response)*

Reader 7: Come, Holy Spirit, when we need to show respect for other people and for the world around us. *(Response)*

Reader 8: Come, Holy Spirit, when we need to be reminded of how great God's world and God's people really are. *(Response)*

Leader: Come Holy Spirit, fill the hearts of your faithful.
Enkindle in us the fire of your love.
Send forth your Spirit and we shall be created.
And you shall renew the face of the earth.

In the name of the Father, and of the Son and of the Holy Spirit.

All: Amen.

Closing Hymn: ♪ *Spirit-Filled Day* (Track 26)

5. Pentecost

Term 3

6. The Holy Trinity

For the Leader: The Solemnity of the Most Holy Trinity is celebrated on the Sunday after Pentecost Sunday. It follows in a series of feast days which begins with Ascension Sunday and ends with Corpus Christi. The Feast of the Most Holy Trinity celebrates the central mystery of Christian faith and life; namely our belief in One God in three persons: Father, Son and Holy Spirit. Many great theologians have tried and failed to explain fully the mystery of the Holy Trinity. Indeed, St Jerome famously said, 'The true profession of the mystery of the Trinity is to own that we do not comprehend it.' This prayer assembly will use words and images to help children to understand the unity of three persons in One God.

> **You will need:**
> - Six children to read
> - Three large bowls
> - Kettle of hot water
> - Jug of cold water
> - Some ice
> - Two children to hold bowls of cold water and ice
> - One adult to hold a bowl of hot water
>
> **Sacred Space:**
> - White cloth
> - Bible
> - Candle
> - Cross/Crucifix
> - Shamrock

Opening Song: ♪ *Bless The Lord (Glory Be To The Father)* (Track 5)

Leader: In the name of the Father, and of the Son and of the Holy Spirit.

All: Amen.

Leader: Let us begin with our Prayer to the Holy Spirit:

All: Holy Spirit, I want to do what is right. Help me.
Holy Spirit, I want to live like Jesus. Guide me.
Holy Spirit, I want to pray like Jesus. Teach me. Amen.

Leader: We begin all of our prayers in the name of (i) the Father, and (ii) of the Son and (iii) of the Holy Spirit. When we do this, we are saying that we believe that there are three persons in one God: there is God the Father, who created the world; God the Son, Jesus Christ; and God the Holy Spirit, who lives with us now and who helps us to live as Jesus asks us to. This unity of three persons in one is called the Holy Trinity.

The Holy Trinity is one of those things that we cannot fully understand. However, we can see signs and symbols from God's world to help us to work it out. So, let's see if we can use the gift of water to help us to understand the Holy Trinity.

Reader 1: Let's imagine God the Father is like water. Water is the most basic element that exists. It gives life to everything.

Child pours the jug of water into a bowl

Reader 2: Let's imagine Jesus is like ice. Ice comes from water. It cannot exist without water. Eventually, it will go back to being water.

Child puts some ice into a bowl

Reader 3: Let's imagine the Holy Spirit is like steam. Steam comes from hot water. It cannot exist without water.

Adult pours the kettle of water into a bowl, and allows the steam to rise

Leader: Water, ice and steam are all related. In fact, they are all the same, but they are also all different. In the same way, God the Father, God the Son and God the Holy Spirit are the same God, but they are three separate persons. Every week at Mass we say that we believe in all three when we pray the Creed. Let us listen closely to the words of this prayer now, and what they tell us about each person in the Holy Trinity:

Reader 4: I believe in one God, the Father almighty,
maker of heaven and earth,
of all things visible and invisible.

Reader 5: I believe in one Lord Jesus Christ,
the Only Begotten Son of God,
born of the Father before all ages.
God from God, Light from Light,
true God from true God,
begotten, not made, consubstantial
with the Father;
Through him all things were made.
For us men and for our salvation
he came down from heaven,
and by the Holy Spirit was incarnate
of the Virgin Mary,
and became man.

For our sake he was crucified
under Pontius Pilate,
he suffered death and was buried,
and rose again on the third day
in accordance with the Scriptures.
He ascended into heaven
and is seated at the right hand of the Father.
He will come again in glory
to judge the living and the dead
and his kingdom will have no end.

Reader 6: I believe in the Holy Spirit,
the Lord, the giver of life,
who proceeds from the Father and the Son,
who with the Father and the Son
is adored and glorified,
who has spoken through the prophets.

Leader: Together, let us profess our belief in the Holy Trinity:

All: Glory be to the Father .../ *Glóir don Athair* ...

Leader: In the name of the Father, and of the Son and of the Holy Spirit.

All: Amen.

Closing Hymn: ♪ *All The Nations Of The Earth*
(Track 2)

Term 3

7. The Body and Blood of Christ (Corpus Christi)

For the Leader: The Feast of the Body and Blood of Christ (Corpus Christi) is celebrated on the Sunday after Trinity Sunday. On this day, we remember and celebrate the gift of the Eucharist. As Catholics, we believe that Jesus is really present under the appearances of bread and wine that we share when we receive Holy Communion. We believe this because of what Jesus said at the Last Supper – 'This is my Body' ... This is my Blood' ... Do this in memory of me.' People celebrate the Feast of the Body and Blood of Christ by attending Mass and sometimes by taking part in Corpus Christi processions. If such a procession is planned in your parish, let the children know and encourage them to go.

> **You will need:**
> - Six children to read
>
> **Sacred Space:**
> - White cloth
> - Bible, open at 1 Corinthians 11:23-25
> - Candle
> - Cross/Crucifix
> - Bread and wine or a cup and plate
> - Flour and grapes

Opening Song: ♪ *Happy In The Presence* (Track 16)

Leader: In the name of the Father, and of the Son and of the Holy Spirit.

All: Amen.

Leader: Let us begin with our Prayer to the Holy Spirit:

All: Holy Spirit, I want to do what is right. Help me.
Holy Spirit, I want to live like Jesus. Guide me.
Holy Spirit, I want to pray like Jesus. Teach me. Amen.

Leader: What we eat is very important. The better the food we eat, the stronger and healthier we become. As we gather together today, we take time to think about a special meal to which we are invited each week. This is a very important meal that will help us to be better people. This is the meal that Jesus shared with his apostles and which he now shares with us. The food that we eat looks like bread and wine but after the consecration it has become the Body and Blood of Jesus. Let us listen to the story of the first celebration of Mass, at the Last Supper:

Reader 1: *A reading from the letter of St Paul to the Corinthians (11:23-25)*
I have already told you what the Lord Jesus did on the night he was betrayed. And it came from the Lord himself. He took some bread in his hands. Then after he had given thanks, he broke it and said,

Reader 2: 'This is my body, which is given for you. Eat this and remember me.'

Reader 1: After the meal, Jesus took a cup of wine in his hands and said,

Reader 2: 'This is my blood, and with it God makes his new agreement with you. Drink this and remember me.'

Reader 1: The Word of the Lord.

All: Thanks be to God.

♪ *Play 'Eat This Bread'* (Track 13) *and encourage the children to sing along*

Leader: When we receive the Bread of Life, it is Jesus we receive. He becomes part of us in a very special way. If Jesus is a part of us, we must try to live as he wants us to. We must be kind to others. We must show love. We must share the gifts that we have been given. Let us ask Jesus to help us to do these things. The response to each prayer is, 'I am happy in the presence of the Lord.'

All: I am happy in the presence of the Lord.

Reader 3: When I receive Jesus, the Bread of Life, I share his gift of love with others. (*Response*)

Reader 4: When I receive Jesus, the Bread of Life, I share his gift of forgiveness with others. (*Response*)

Reader 5: When I receive Jesus, the Bread of Life, I share his gift of kindness with others. (*Response*)

Reader 6: When I receive Jesus, the Bread of Life, I share his gift of joy with others. (*Response*)

Leader: Together, let us pray our prayer after Holy Communion together, in thanksgiving for all the times that Jesus, the Bread of Life, has come into our lives.

All: Lord Jesus, I love and adore you.
You're a special friend to me.
Welcome Lord Jesus, O welcome.
Thank you for coming to me.

Thank you, Lord Jesus, O thank you,
For giving yourself to me.
Make me strong to show your love
Wherever I may be.

Be near me, Lord Jesus, I ask you to stay
Close by me forever and love me, I pray.
Bless all of us children in your loving care
And bring me to heaven to live with you there.

I'm ready now, Lord Jesus,
To show how much I care.
I'm ready now to give your love
At home and everywhere. Amen.

Leader: Let us pray:

Jesus, our friend,
you promised to be with us always.
Thank you for the gift of Holy Communion.
Help us to share the love and goodness we receive
with each other.
We make this prayer through Christ, our Lord.

All: Amen.

Leader: In the name of the Father, and of the Son and of the Holy Spirit.

All: Amen.

Closing Hymn: ♪ *Go Now In Peace* (Track 14)

7. The Body and Blood of Christ (Corpus Christi)

Term 3

8. Sacred Heart of Jesus

For the Leader: The Solemnity of the Most Sacred Heart of Jesus is celebrated on the Friday after Corpus Christi. However, the whole month of June is traditionally devoted to the Sacred Heart. While the image of Jesus' exposed heart crowned with thorns comes to mind almost immediately when we think of this feast day, that is quite a modern depiction of what is actually a very old tradition. The Feast of the Sacred Heart of Jesus recalls God's immense love, which came to life in the person of Jesus. In the words of St Paul, ' ... neither death nor life, neither angels nor demons, neither the present nor the future, nor any powers, neither height nor depth, nor anything else in all creation, will be able to separate us from the love of God that is in Christ Jesus our Lord' (Romans 8:38-39). That is what we want to communicate to our school community through this prayer service.

> **You will need:**
> - Eight children to read
>
> **Sacred Space:**
> - White cloth
> - Bible, open at Matthew 20:19-34, 14:13-14 and John 11:1-43
> - Candle
> - Cross/Crucifix
> - An image of the Sacred Heart of Jesus

Opening Song: ♪ *Christ Is My Light* (Track 8)

Leader: In the name of the Father, and of the Son and of the Holy Spirit.

All: Amen.

Leader: Let us begin with our Prayer to the Holy Spirit:

All: Holy Spirit, I want to do what is right. Help me.
Holy Spirit, I want to live like Jesus. Guide me.
Holy Spirit, I want to pray like Jesus. Teach me. Amen.

Leader: We gather together today to celebrate the Feast of the Sacred Heart of Jesus. The word 'sacred' means 'holy' or 'blessed'. Why do you think we call Jesus' heart 'sacred'? (*Invite children to think in silence or to answer aloud, whichever is most appropriate*)

Jesus' heart was 'sacred' because it was filled with love for everyone he met. Let's remind ourselves of some of the times when Jesus showed his 'sacred heart'.

Reader 1: One day, two blind men were sitting at the side of a road. When they heard that Jesus was coming their way, they shouted, 'Lord and Son of David, have pity on us!' The crowd told them to be quiet, but they shouted even louder, 'Lord and Son of David, have pity on us!' When Jesus heard them, he stopped and asked, 'What do you want me to do for you?' They answered, 'Lord, we want to see!' Jesus felt sorry for them and touched their eyes. Right away they could see, and they became his followers. (*Matthew 20:19-34*)

Reader 2: When Jesus heard about the death of his cousin, John the Baptist, he got into a boat and crossed the Sea of Galilee to go to some place where he could be alone. But the people found out where he was going and followed him. When Jesus got out of the boat, he saw the large crowd. Even though he was sad and tired himself, he felt sorry for the people and so he healed everyone who was sick. (*Matthew 14:13-14*)

Reader 3: Jesus had three good friends called Mary, Martha and Lazarus, who lived in a town called Bethany. One day, word reached Jesus that Lazarus was very sick, but Jesus did not go to see him right away, because he thought he would get better. By the time Jesus reached Bethany, two days later, Lazarus was dead. When he saw Mary and Martha, and how upset there were at Lazarus' death, Jesus began to cry too. He asked to be brought to the tomb where Lazarus was buried. There, Jesus prayed to God, and when he had finished, he shouted 'Lazarus, come out!', and Lazarus came out of the tomb. (*John 11:1-43*)

Leader: In each of these stories, we hear that Jesus felt sorry for the people who were suffering, and he shared in their sadness. These are times when Jesus showed us his 'sacred heart.' Jesus' sacred heart is still moved when people are unhappy, lonely or afraid. He is still with us, comforting us, especially during those times when we are most in need. Let us pray to Jesus now, trusting that his heart is full of love for us. The response to each prayer is, 'Sacred heart of Jesus, I place all my trust in you'.

All: Sacred heart of Jesus, I place all my trust in you.

Reader 4: Sacred heart of Jesus, pour out your love on those who are sick at home or in hospital. (*Response*)

Reader 5: Sacred heart of Jesus, pour out your love on people who do not have enough food to eat, or do not have homes to live in. (*Response*)

Reader 6: Sacred heart of Jesus, pour out your love on those who are lonely, and have no one to visit them. (*Response*)

Reader 7: Sacred heart of Jesus, pour out your love on those who live in places of war, conflict and violence. (*Response*)

Reader 8: Sacred heart of Jesus, pour out your love on all of us gathered here today, so that we can help to bring your goodness to the world. (*Response*)

Leader: Let us pray:

Jesus, our friend,
Your sacred heart was full of love for the people you met.
It is still full of love for all people, and especially those who are in need.
Help us, your followers, to show our care for those who need help.
Pour out your love on us.
We make this prayer through Christ our Lord.

All: Amen.

Leader: In the name of the Father, and of the Son and of the Holy Spirit.

All: Amen.

Closing Hymn: ♪ *Christ Be Our Light* (Track 7)

8. Sacred Heart of Jesus

Term 3

9. End of the School Year

For the Leader: As we come to the end of the school year, it is good to take time to reflect on all that has happened. We thank God for all the blessings our school communities have received, and pray for a safe and happy summer. You may like to amend this prayer service to take into account any special occasions or achievements that were particular to your school this year. Depending on the size of your school, you could invite parents/guardians and grandparents to join you for this gathering. It is important to recognise especially any members of the school community who are leaving this year, including any 6th class students.

> **You will need:**
> - Five children to read
> - A child from each classroom to carry his/her class's candle to the sacred space
> - Four children to carry symbols to the sacred space. One of these children should be from the Junior Infant class
>
> **Sacred Space:**
> - Green cloth
> - Bible, open at John 15:12-17
> - Cross/Crucifix
> - Other items will be added to the sacred space during the service: a picture of the Junior Infant class/es, some books, a Bible, a family picture

Opening Song: ♪ *Circle Of Friends* (Track 9)

During or after the opening song, one student from each classroom could come in procession with their class's candle, which has been used for prayer during the year, and place it in the sacred space. The candles can then be lit.

Leader: In the name of the Father, and of the Son and of the Holy Spirit.

All: Amen.

Leader: Let us begin with our Prayer to the Holy Spirit:

All: Holy Spirit, I want to do what is right. Help me.
Holy Spirit, I want to live like Jesus. Guide me.
Holy Spirit, I want to pray like Jesus. Teach me. Amen.

Leader: We gather together today to thank God for the year that has passed, and to ask his blessing as we look forward to the holidays. When you think about this year in school, what has been the one thing that has stood out for you? What has been your best memory? *(Invite children to think in silence or to answer aloud, whichever is most appropriate)*

One of the best things we can remember, this year or any year, is that we treated each other with love, respect and kindness. When we did that, we showed that we are friends of Jesus. Let us listen to a passage from the Gospel which tells us exactly that:

Reader 1: *A reading from the Holy Gospel according to John (15:12-17)*
Now I tell you to love each other, as I have loved you. The greatest way to show love for friends is to die for them. And you are my friends, if you obey me. Servants don't know what their master is doing, and so I don't speak to you as my servants. I speak to you as my friends, and I have told you everything that my Father has told me. You did not choose me. I chose you and sent you out to produce fruit, the kind of fruit that will last. Then my Father will give you whatever you ask for in my name. So I command you to love each other.

The Gospel of the Lord.

All: Praise to you, Lord Jesus Christ.

Leader: In the past year, every one of you has made our school a better place. We will now take time to reflect on some of the events that happened during the past year, and to thank God for them.

Reader 2: Last September, our school welcomed _____ (*number*) new children into Junior Infants. These students came and brought new life to the classes they joined and to our whole school. (*Pause*)

We bring a picture of our Junior Infant class(es) to the sacred space. (*Pause*)

Child from Junior Infants brings a picture of the Junior Infant class(es) to the sacred space

We give glory and praise to God for them.

Reader 3: This year we learned many new things about God's world. We thank him for our teachers, who have encouraged us to discover and learn. (*Pause*)

We bring some books to the sacred space. (*Pause*)

Child brings some books to the sacred space

We give glory and praise to God for all we have learned.

Reader 4: We have taken time each day this year to pray to God, and to grow in friendship with him. Some students also celebrated the Sacraments of First Reconciliation, First Holy Communion and Confirmation this year. (*Pause*)

We bring a Bible to the sacred space. (*Pause*)

Child brings a Bible to the sacred space

We give glory and praise to God for his presence.

Reader 5: Our parents and families are always our best teachers. We thank them for their love and care this year, and we ask God to bless them.

We bring a family picture to the sacred space. (*Pause*)

Child brings a picture of their family to the sacred space

We give glory and praise to God for our parents and families.

At this point, you may like to mention other significant events that happened during the year – for example, if your school was awarded a Green Flag, or if there was a particular sporting, music or academic achievement.

Leader: We give glory and praise to God for all that has been this year, as together we say:

All: Glory be to the Father …/*Glóir don Athair* …

Leader: We now invite those who are leaving our school community this year to stand. I invite all others to face them, and to raise your right hand in blessing as we send them forth on their journey of life.

Go carefully my dear friends.
May you always know where you have come from, may you always remember that you are cared for, may the gentle hand of God guide you in life's path, and may you always know the love of God in your life.
We make this prayer through Christ our Lord.

All: Amen.

Leader: In the name of the Father, and of the Son and of the Holy Spirit.

All: Amen.

Closing Hymn: ♪ *Christ Be Our Light* (Track 7)

Other Resources

1. For Board of Management/Staff Meetings
a. Beginning of the School Year

> **You will need:**
> - Two people to read
>
> **Sacred Space:**
> - Green cloth
> - Bible, open at Matthew 13:31-32
> - Candle
> - Cross/Crucifix

Leader: In the name of the Father, and of the Son and of the Holy Spirit.

All: Amen.

Leader: We gather together today as we begin a new school year. We thank God for the blessings that the summer break brought, and pray that we will begin this new academic year with energy and hope in our hearts. As a Catholic school, it is appropriate to begin our year with a reading from the Gospel.

Reader 1: *A reading from the Holy Gospel according to Matthew (13:31-32)*
Jesus told them another story: The kingdom of heaven is like what happens when a farmer plants a mustard seed in a field. Although it is the smallest of all seeds, it grows larger than any garden plant and becomes a tree. Birds even come and nest on its branches.

The Gospel of the Lord.

All: Praise to you, Lord Jesus Christ.

Leader: Jesus taught using examples from the world around him. The people to whom he was speaking were farmers, so he used the example of the mustard seed – the smallest of all seeds – to explain to them what the Kingdom of God is like. In our context, we might see the mustard seed mirrored in the children in our school. In this parable, Jesus urges us not to give up on any seed, particularly the smallest. He reminds us that just as the mustard tree has the potential to become the largest tree, so too do all the children in our school have potential beyond anything that we can imagine.

Reader 2: *A Reflection by Bishop Ken Untener*
It helps, now and then, to step back and take a long view.
The kingdom is not only beyond our efforts, it is even beyond our vision.
We accomplish in our lifetime only a tiny fraction of the magnificent enterprise that is God's work. Nothing we do is complete, which is a way of saying that the Kingdom always lies beyond us.

No statement says all that could be said.
No prayer fully expresses our faith.
No confession brings perfection.
No pastoral visit brings wholeness.
No programme accomplishes the Church's mission.
No set of goals and objectives includes everything.

This is what we are about.

We plant the seeds that one day will grow.
We water seeds already planted, knowing that they hold future promise.
We lay foundations that will need further development.
We provide yeast that produces far beyond our capabilities.

We cannot do everything, and there is a sense of liberation in realising that.
This enables us to do something, and to do it very well.
It may be incomplete, but it is a beginning, a step along the way, an opportunity for the Lord's grace to enter and do the rest.
We may never see the end results, but that is the difference between the master builder and the worker.
We are workers, not master builders; ministers, not messiahs.
We are prophets of a future not our own.

Leader: Let us take comfort in these words. We could not do everything last year, we cannot do everything this year, and we will not do everything next year! But we can 'do something, and do it very well'. We ask for God's grace and help to do that something, in his name, this year. Let us pray together:

All: Our Father .../*Ár nAthair* ...

Leader: In the name of the Father, and of the Son and of the Holy Spirit.

All: Amen.

1. For Board of Management/Staff Meetings

Other Resources

1. For Board of Management/Staff Meetings
b. Advent/Christmas

> **You will need:**
> - Two people to read
>
> **Sacred Space:**
> - Violet cloth
> - Bible, open at John 3:16-17
> - An Advent Wreath, with the correct number of candles lighting, depending on the week in which the prayer service is being celebrated
> - Cross/Crucifix

Leader: In the name of the Father, and of the Son and of the Holy Spirit.

All: Amen.

Leader: We gather together today in the season of Advent. It is a season of waiting and of preparing; a time of hope. The children in our school are excited about Santa and about presents, and sometimes it can seem that we are the only ones reminding them of the 'real' meaning of Christmas. But what is the 'real' meaning of Christmas? What difference does its celebration make?

Reader 1: *An account from a soldier in the trenches, 1914**
We had a rather interesting time in the trenches on Christmas Eve and Christmas Day. We were in some places less than a hundred yards from the Germans, and we talked to them. It was agreed in our part of the firing line that there would be no firing and no thought of war on these days, so they sang and played several songs for us, while we did the same for them.

The soldiers on our left got out of their trenches and every time a flare went up they simply stood there, cheered and waved their hats, and not a shot was fired on them. On Christmas Eve the Germans burnt coloured lights and candles all along the tops of their trenches and the singing and playing continued all night. On Christmas Day we paid a visit to the German trenches and swapped cigarettes with each other and one of the German officers took photos of us all, arm in arm. We wore their helmets and they wore ours. They allowed us to bury our dead in peace and they even brought one of our soldiers from behind their trench so that we could bury him with the others. On December 26, both sides starting fighting again, but, because of Christmas, they had a different understanding of their enemy.

Leader: This story, whether historically accurate or not, gives us a sense of the potential of Christmas, and the possibilities that lie within it. Christmas is an opportunity for peace not just between fighting nations, but between family and friends, and even within ourselves. As the Gospel according to St John reminds us, that is why Jesus came into the world.

Reader 2: *A reading from the Holy Gospel according to John (3:16-17)*
God loved the people of this world so much that he gave his only Son, so that everyone who has faith in him will have eternal life and never really die. God did not send his Son into the world to condemn its people. He sent him to save them!

The Gospel of the Lord.

All: Praise to you, Lord Jesus Christ.

Leader: We pray that the potential offered by this holy season will be realised in our home, school and parish communities, as together we pray:

All: Our Father .../Ár nAthair ...

Leader: In the name of the Father, and of the Son and of the Holy Spirit.

All: Amen.

---
*Alive-O 7, p. 102.

Other Resources

1. For Board of Management/Staff Meetings
c. End of the School Year

You will need:
- One person to read
- A copy of the blessing on page 101 for each person

Sacred Space:
- Green cloth
- Bible, open at Mark 4:2-9
- Candle
- Cross/Crucifix

Leader: In the name of the Father, and of the Son and of the Holy Spirit.

All: Amen.

Leader: We gather together today for our final meeting of this school year. We thank God for the blessings we experienced this year, and for his presence with us in those days that were most difficult. Let us reflect on our time together this year using the Parable of the Sower.

Reader 1: *A reading from the Holy Gospel according to Mark (4:2-9)*
A farmer went out to scatter seed in a field. While the farmer was scattering the seed, some of it fell along the road and was eaten by birds. Other seeds fell on thin, rocky ground and quickly started growing because the soil wasn't very deep. But when the sun came up, the plants were scorched and dried up, because they did not have enough roots. Some other seeds fell where thornbushes grew up and choked out the plants. So they did not produce any grain. But a few seeds did fall on good ground where the plants grew and produced thirty or sixty or even a hundred times as much as was scattered.

The Gospel of the Lord.

All: Praise to you, Lord Jesus Christ.

Leader: We planted many seeds in our school this year, and they fell on all sorts of ground! Let's take a moment to reflect on the year, and to ask ourselves these questions:

1. Where did seeds grow in our school this year? What were our successes? (*Pause*)

2. Where did seeds fall on thin, rocky ground? What were our greatest challenges? (*Pause*)

You may like to give everyone a moment to think quietly, and then invite them to share with the person next to them, or with the whole group.

Leader: We remember our successes with thanksgiving and our challenges with consolation as together we pray:

All: Our Father .../Ár nAthair ...

Leader: Let us finish with a blessing for each other, and for the work that we do.

All: May God reward the work that we have done in building this school community in his name. May we enjoy the health and energy to continue in our vocation.

May he bless those whom we have served. Together, may we strive to live our lives in love for him and for others.

May we have a restful break from school life, and return refreshed and renewed. Until then, may God bless us and those whom we love.

Amen.

Leader: In the name of the Father, and of the Son and of the Holy Spirit.

All: Amen.

May God reward the work that we have done in building this school community in his name. May we enjoy the health and energy to continue in our vocation.

May he bless those whom we have served. Together, may we strive to live our lives in love for him and for others.

May we have a restful break from school life, and return refreshed and renewed. Until then, may God bless us and those whom we love.

Amen.

May God reward the work that we have done in building this school community in his name. May we enjoy the health and energy to continue in our vocation.

May he bless those whom we have served. Together, may we strive to live our lives in love for him and for others.

May we have a restful break from school life, and return refreshed and renewed. Until then, may God bless us and those whom we love.

Amen.

Other Resources

2. Remembering our School's Founder

For the Leader: Many schools in Ireland were founded by religious congregations. These congregations were often established for a particular purpose, but all had the common ground of living out the mission of Jesus Christ. The following prayer assembly can be adapted to allow for the school community to come together to remember and celebrate your school's founder. Founders of Religious Orders who established Irish Catholic primary schools include, but are not limited to:

- Nano Nagle, founder of the Presentation Sisters
- Catherine McAuley, founder of the Sisters of Mercy
- Edmund Rice, founder of the Christian Brothers
- Don Bosco, founder of the Salesian Brothers and Sisters
- Louis Marie Eugene Bautain, founder of the Sisters of St Louis
- Claude Poullart des Places and Francis Liberman, founders of the Spiritian Fathers

---

You will need:
- Eight children to read
- The life-story of your school's founder

Sacred Space:
- White cloth
- Bible, open at Matthew 19:13-14
- Candle
- Cross/Crucifix
- Image of the school founder
- School Crest

Opening Song: ♪ *This Is The Day* (Track 30)

Leader: In the name of the Father, and of the Son and of the Holy Spirit.

All: Amen.

Leader: We gather together today to remember a person who is very important to our school, _____. He/She felt that it was important that all people are able to read and write and for this reason he/she set up a school. He/She was also a person who had come to know Jesus in a very special way and who wanted to share that with others.

Reader 1: *The life-story of your school's founder*

Leader: _____ was influenced by the Word of God and so we take time to listen to that Word.

Reader 2: *A reading from the Holy Gospel according to Matthew (19:13-14)*
Some people brought their children to Jesus, so that he could place his hands on them and pray for them. His disciples told the people to stop bothering him. But Jesus said, 'Let the children come to me, and don't try to stop them! People who are like these children belong to God's kingdom.'

The Gospel of the Lord.

All: Praise to you, Lord Jesus Christ.

Leader: Jesus invited the children to come and sit with him, and he blessed them. We now make our prayers to him, knowing that he has a special love for children. The response to each of our prayers is: Lord, hear our prayer.

All: Lord, hear our prayer.

Reader 3: We pray in thanksgiving for the vision of _____, whose Religious Order founded our school. It is because of him/her that many people have had the gift of education. May we keep his/her spirit alive in our school. We pray to the Lord. (*Response*)

Reader 4: We pray for the members of the _____ community who have worked in our school over the past _____ years. May the Lord bless them for all the great work that they have done. We pray to the Lord. (*Response*)

Reader 5: We pray for the members of the _____ community who work in the developing world today, trying to bring a better life to people through education. May the Lord strengthen them in their work. We pray to the Lord. (*Response*)

Reader 6: We pray for vocations to the _____ community. May men/ women be inspired by the life of_____ and so follow in their footsteps to build up the Kingdom of God in our time. We pray to the Lord. (*Response*)

Reader 7: We pray that all here in _____ school will follow the example of _____ . We pray to the Lord. (*Response*)

Reader 8: We pray for the members of the _____ community who have died. May they be rewarded for their dedication to Catholic schools such as ours. We pray to the Lord. (*Response*)

Leader: Together, let us give glory to God, as _____ did:

All: Glory be to the Father .../*Glóir don Athair* ...

Leader: Let us pray:

Loving God,
You called _____ to bring the Good News of Jesus to others.
Help us to listen to your voice in our lives.
We make this prayer through Christ our Lord.

All: Amen.

Leader: In the name of the Father, and of the Son and of the Holy Spirit.

All: Amen.

Closing Song: ♪ *Christ Be Beside Me* (Track 6)

2. Remembering our School's Founder

Other Resources

3. At a Time of Illness

For the Leader: In the life of a school, some member of staff, student, parent or priest may become seriously sick. The following prayer assembly can be adapted to allow for the school community to come together to pray for the gift of healing for that person.

> **You will need:**
> - A 'Get Well' book or card for the person who is sick, which all or some of the school community have signed
> - Eight children to read
> - One child to carry the 'Get Well' book or card to the sacred space
>
> **Sacred Space:**
> - White cloth
> - Bible, open at Luke 17:11-19
> - Candle
> - Cross/Crucifix
> - Holy water
> - Name or picture of the person who is sick

Opening Song: ♪ *Christ Be Beside Me* (Track 6)

Leader: In the name of the Father, and of the Son and of the Holy Spirit.

All: Amen.

Leader: We have often reflected on Jesus as one who heals. He healed the ten lepers, Simon Peter's mother-in-law, the man who was paralysed, the man who was blind, and many, many others. Aware that Jesus has the power to heal, we gather together today to ask him to bless _____ , who is sick at this time. As we begin, let's close our eyes and in the silence of our hearts, we will ask Jesus to give healing to _____ . *(Pause)*

We now place our 'Get Well' book/card in the sacred space.

Child places the 'Get Well' book/card in the sacred space.

Leader: Let us listen to a healing story from the Gospel according to Luke (*17:11-19*)

Reader 1: On his way to Jerusalem, Jesus went along the border between Samaria and Galilee. As he was going into a village, ten men with leprosy came toward him. They stood at a distance and shouted,

Reader 2: 'Jesus, Master, have pity on us!'

Reader 1: Jesus looked at them and said,

Reader 3: 'Go show yourselves to the priests.'

Reader 1: On their way they were healed. When one of them discovered that he was healed, he came back, shouting praises to God. He bowed down at the feet of Jesus and thanked him. The man was from the country of Samaria. Jesus asked,

Reader 3: 'Weren't ten men healed? Where are the other nine? Why was this foreigner the only one who came back to thank God?'

Reader 1: Then Jesus told the man,

Reader 3: 'You may get up and go. Your faith has made you well.'

Reader 1: The Gospel of the Lord.

All: Praise to you, Lord Jesus Christ.

Leader: Jesus, the healer, had pity on the lepers who were sick, and made them well again. Let us offer our prayers to him, knowing that he always listens to us. The response to each of these prayers is, 'Lord, graciously hear us'.

All: Lord, graciously hear us.

Reader 4: We pray for _____ , who is sick at this time. May Jesus the healer be with him/her. Lord, hear us. *(Response)*

Reader 5: We pray for _____ 's family. May God strengthen them at this difficult time. Lord, hear us. (*Response*)

Reader 6: We pray for all who are taking care of _____ while he/she is unwell. May God bless them in their work. Lord, hear us. (*Response*)

Reader 7: We pray for all who are sick and afraid. May they always remember that God loves and cares for them, especially when they are sick. Lord, hear us. (*Response*)

Reader 8: We pray for all those gathered here. May we always bring comfort to those who are sick. Lord, hear us. (*Response*)

Leader: We take a moment to remember anyone else we know who is sick at this time. *Pause for a moment.* Lord, hear us. (*Response*)

Leader: We bring all our prayers for _____ together as we ask Mary, our Mother, to watch over him/her in this time of sickness.

All: Hail Mary .../*'Sé do bheatha, a Mhuire ...*

Leader: Let us pray:

Loving God,
We know that you are with us always and that you are with _____ , who is sick.
We trust that, as you shared your gift of healing with those you met while you lived among us, you will share it with _____ today.
We make this prayer through Christ our Lord.

All: Amen.

Leader: In the name of the Father, and of the Son and of the Holy Spirit.

All: Amen.

Closing Song: ♪ *Christ Be Our Light* (Track 7)

Other Resources

4. On the Death of a Student

For the Leader: The death of a student is an absolute tragedy for any school community. This may be children's first experience of death, and the death of their friend, is undoubtedly traumatic. One of the ways that the school community can respond to this great loss is by turning to its faith tradition in prayer. The following prayer service is designed to be used on the death of a student, and can be adapted to fit the needs of your school community.

> **You will need:**
> - Memory Tree: Either a bare branch secured in sand in a vase, pot or bowl, or the outline of a tree or branch drawn on a banner, noticeboard or large piece of card/paper
> - One prayer leaf for each person. The template for this leaf is on page 27. Invite the students to write the name of the student who has died on one side and to write or draw something that reminds them of the person on the other. These should be completed before the prayer assembly begins, and placed on the Memory Tree. One child from each class can keep their prayer leaf as they will add it to the tree during the service
> - A hole-puncher and some string to attach the prayer leaves to the Memory Tree
> - Five children to read
> - One child from each class to place their prayer leaf on the Memory Tree
>
> **Sacred Space:**
> - White cloth
> - Bible, open at Mark 10:13-16
> - Candle
> - Cross/Crucifix
> - Name or picture of the person who has died

Opening Song: ♪ *Remember Them* (Track 23)

Leader: In the name of the Father, and of the Son and of the Holy Spirit.

All: Amen.

Leader: We gather together today in sadness at _____ 's death. _____ was part of our school community and we all have very special memories of him/her. In this prayer service we are going to take time to share our memories and to pray that _____ will be welcomed into Jesus' home in heaven and be among God's angels. We will also pray for _____ 's family who are very sad at this time. We will ask Jesus to be with them. Let us listen to what Jesus had to say about children:

Reader 1: *A reading from the Holy Gospel according to Mark (10:13-16)*
Some people brought their children to Jesus so that he could bless them by placing his hands on them. But his disciples told the people to stop bothering him.
   When Jesus saw this, he became angry and said, 'Let the children come to me! Don't try to stop them. People who are like these little children belong to the kingdom of God. I promise you that you cannot get into God's kingdom, unless you accept it the way a child does.' Then Jesus took the children in his arms and blessed them by placing his hands on them.

The Gospel of the Lord.

All: Praise to you, Lord Jesus Christ.

Leader: In the Gospel we see how Jesus loved children and how he took them in his arms and blessed them. We know that Jesus loves _____ very much and is holding him/her in his arms, just like in the Gospel story. Let us now take some time to remember _____ .

♪ *Play Reflective Music* (Track 22) *and read the following meditation slowly:*

Close your eyes for a moment. Be as quiet and still as you can. Now imagine Jesus walking towards you. He comes and sits beside you. Tell him how you're feeling today. *(Pause)*

Tell Jesus about _____, who has died. Describe him/her to Jesus. Tell Jesus about a happy time you shared together. Ask Jesus to bless _____.
Listen to what Jesus has to say. (*Pause*)

It's now time for you to leave Jesus, although you know he's always with you. (*Pause*)

When you're ready, you can open your eyes.

We all have great memories of _____, and earlier, we took time to write or draw these for our Memory Tree. At the start the tree was bare and not very bright. Now, with most of the leaves on it, it looks a lot better. We now invite one person from each class to place their leaves on the tree, representing all of our memories of _____.

You may like these children to come forward all together, or to call them one-by-one

Leader: Jesus loves children very much and we are sure that he always listens to our prayers. The response to each of these prayers is, 'Lord, graciously hear us.'

All: Lord, graciously hear us.

Reader 2: Jesus, you welcomed children and promised them your Kingdom. We hope that our friend _____ will be happy in his/her new home in heaven, safe in the company of God's angels. Lord, hear us. (*Response*)

Reader 3: Jesus, you comforted those who were sad. May you comfort the family of _____ who are very sad at this time. Lord, hear us. (*Response*)

Reader 4: Jesus, you cared for the sick. May you bless all those who cared for _____ when he/she needed it. Lord, hear us. (*Response*)

Reader 5: Jesus, you were a friend of children. May we feel your love today, at this time of great sadness. Lord, hear us. (*Response*)

Leader: _____ is now among God's angels, and so we bring all our prayers together as we pray to our Guardian Angel.

All: Angel sent by God to guide me,
be my light and walk beside me;
be my guardian and protect me;
on the paths of life direct me.
Amen.

Leader: Let us pray:

Loving God,
_____ did not stay with us for very long.
We thank you for the gift that he/she was to his/her family and to our school.
May he/she now rest peacefully in heaven and watch over us from there.
We make this our prayer through Christ our Lord.

All: Amen.

Leader: In the name of the Father, and of the Son and of the Holy Spirit.

All: Amen

Closing Song: ♪ *Close To You* (Track 10)

4. On the Death of a Student

Other Resources

5. On the Death of a Staff Member

For the Leader: The loss of a staff member is devastating for any school community. One of the ways that the school community can respond to this great loss is by turning to its faith tradition in prayer. The following prayer service is designed to be used on the death of a staff member, and can be adapted to fit the needs of your school community.

> **You will need:**
> - Memory Tree: Either a bare branch secured in sand in a vase, pot or bowl, or the outline of a tree or branch drawn on a banner, noticeboard or large piece of card/paper
> - One prayer leaf for each person. The template for this leaf is on page 27. Invite the students to write the name of the staff member who has died on one side and to write or draw something that reminds them of the person on the other. These should be completed before the prayer assembly begins, and placed on the Memory Tree. One child from each class can keep their prayer leaf as they will add it to the tree during the service
> - A hole-puncher and some string to attach the prayer leaves to the Memory Tree
> - Five children to read
> - One child from each class to place their prayer leaf on the Memory Tree
>
> **Sacred Space:**
> - White cloth
> - Bible, open at John 14:1-6
> - Candle
> - Cross/Crucifix
> - Name or picture of the person who has died

Opening Song: ♪ *Remember Them* (Track 23)

Leader: In the name of the Father, and of the Son and of the Holy Spirit.

All: Amen.

Leader: We gather together today in sadness at _____'s death. _____ was part of our school community and we all have very special memories of him/her. In this prayer service we are going to take time to share our memories and to pray that _____ will be welcomed into Jesus' home in heaven. We will also pray for _____'s family who are very sad at this time. We will ask Jesus to be with them. Let us listen to what Jesus had to say about people who die:

Reader 1: *A reading from the Holy Gospel according to John (14:1-6)*
Jesus said to his disciples, 'Don't be worried! Have faith in God and have faith in me. There are many rooms in my Father's house. I wouldn't tell you this, unless it was true. I am going there to prepare a place for each of you. After I have done this, I will come back and take you with me. Then we will be together. You know the way to where I am going.' Thomas said, 'Lord, we don't even know where you are going! How can we know the way?' 'I am the way, the truth, and the life!' Jesus answered. 'Without me, no one can go to the Father.'

The Gospel of the Lord.

All: Praise to you, Lord Jesus Christ.

Leader: Jesus said that he is the way, the truth, and the life. If we follow his way, we will get to live with him in heaven forever. _____ followed the way of Jesus in his/her life, and so we can be sure that he/she is with God in heaven. Let us think about our best memories of _____ now.

What word would you use to describe _____? (*Invite children to think in their head or to answer aloud, whichever is most appropriate*)

Can you remember something you learned from him/her? (*Invite children to think in silence or to answer aloud, whichever is most appropriate*)

I know that we all have great memories of _____, and earlier we took time to write or draw these for our Memory Tree. At the start the tree was bare and not very bright. Now, with most of the leaves on it, it looks a lot better. We now invite one person from each class to place their leaves on the tree, representing all of our memories of _____.

You may like these children to come forward all together, or to call them one-by-one

Leader: Jesus is the way to the Father in heaven, so we now make our prayers to him. The response to each of these prayers is, 'Lord, graciously hear us.'

All: Lord, graciously hear us.

Reader 2: Jesus, you are the way to the Father. May you reward _____ for all the time that he/she gave to teaching children about you. Lord, hear us. (*Response*)

Reader 3: Jesus, you comforted those who were sad. May you comfort the family of _____ who are very sad at this time. Lord, hear us. (*Response*)

Reader 4: Jesus, you cared for the sick. May you bless all those who cared for _____ when he/she needed it. Lord, hear us. (*Response*)

Reader 5: Jesus, you were a friend of children. May we feel your love today, at this time of great sadness. Lord, hear us. (*Response*)

Leader: Let us pray:

Loving God,
We thank you for the life of _____, who was a wonderful part of our school community.
We know that he/she is now at home with you in heaven.
Bless those of us who miss him/her, and help us to remember that, one day, we will all be together in your home.
We make this prayer through Christ, our Lord.

All: Amen.

Leader: In the name of the Father, and of the Son and of the Holy Spirit.

All: Amen.

Closing Song: ♪ *Close To You* (Track 10)

5. On the Death of a Staff Member

Prayer Section

The Sign of the Cross
In the name of the Father, and of the Son
and of the Holy Spirit. Amen.

Comhartha na Croise
In ainm an Athar, agus an Mhic
agus an Spioraid Naoimh. Áiméan.
~

Our Father
Our Father, who art in heaven
Hallowed be thy name.
Thy kingdom come,
Thy will be done
On earth as it is in heaven.
Give us this day our daily bread
And forgive us our trespasses
As we forgive those who trespass against us.
And lead us not into temptation
But deliver us from evil. Amen.

An Phaidir
Ár nAthair atá ar neamh,
Go naofar d'ainm,
Go dtaga do ríocht,
Go ndéantar do thoil ar an talamh
Mar a dhéantar ar neamh.
Ár n-arán laethúil tabhair dúinn inniu,
Agus maith dúinn ár bhfiacha,
Mar a mhaithimidne dár bhféichiúna féin,
Agus ná lig sinn i gcathú,
Ach saor sinn ó olc. Áiméan.
~

Hail Mary
Hail Mary, full of grace,
The Lord is with thee.
Blessed art thou among women
And blessed is the fruit of thy womb, Jesus.
Holy Mary, mother of God,
Pray for us sinners,
Now, and at the hour of our death. Amen.

Sé do Bheatha, a Mhuire
Sé do bheatha, a Mhuire,
Atá lán de ghrásta,
Tá an Tiarna leat.
Is beannaithe thú idir mhná,
Agus is beannaithe toradh do bhroinne, Íosa.
A Naomh Mhuire, a mháthair Dé,
Guigh orainn, na peacaigh,
Anois agus ar uair ár mbáis. Áiméan.
~

Glory be to the Father
Glory be to the Father,
And to the Son,
And to the Holy Spirit;
As it was in the beginning,
Is now and ever shall be,
World without end. Amen.

Glóir don Athair
Glóir don Athair,
Agus don Mhac,
Agus don Spiorad Naomh.
Mar a bhí ó thús,
Mar atá anois,
Mar a bheas go brách,
Le saol na saol. Áiméan.
~

Morning Prayer
Father in heaven, you love me,
You are with me night and day.
I want to love you always
In all I do and say.
I'll try to please you, Father.
Bless me through the day. Amen.
~

Night Prayer
God, our Father, I come to say
Thank you for your love today.
Thank you for my family,
And all the friends you give to me.
Guard me in the dark of night,
And in the morning send your light. Amen.

Prayer to Guardian Angel
Angel sent by God to guide me,
be my light and walk beside me;
be my guardian and protect me;
on the paths of life direct me.
Amen.
~

Prayer to Jesus
Christ be with me.
Christ be beside me.
Christ be before me.
Christ be behind me.
Christ at my right hand.
Christ at my left hand.
Christ be with me everywhere I go.
Christ be my friend, for ever and ever. Amen.

Paidir d'Íosa
Críost liom.
Críost romham.
Críost i mo dhiaidh.
Críost ionam.
Críost ar mo dheis.
Críost ar mo chlé.
Críost i mo chuideachta is cuma cá dtéim.
Críost mar chara agam, anois is go buan. Áiméan.
~

The Angelus
The angel of the Lord declared unto Mary …
And she conceived by the Holy Spirit.
Hail Mary …

Behold the handmaid of the Lord …
Be it done unto me according to thy word.
Hail Mary …

And the Word was made flesh…
And dwelt among us.
Hail Mary …

Pray for us, O holy Mother of God …
That we may be made worthy of the promises of Christ.

Lord,
fill our hearts with your love,
and as you revealed to us by an angel
the coming of your Son as man,
so lead us through his suffering and death
to the glory of his resurrection,
for he lives and reigns with you and the Holy Spirit,
one God, for ever and ever. Amen.

Prayer to the Holy Spirit
Holy Spirit, I want to do what is right. Help me.
Holy Spirit, I want to live like Jesus. Guide me.
Holy Spirit, I want to pray like Jesus. Teach me. Amen.
~

Act of Faith
O my God,
I believe in you
And in all that your holy Church teaches
Because you have said it
And your Word is true.
You are the Christ, the Son of the living God.
You are my Lord and my God.
Lord, I believe; increase my faith.
~

Act of Hope
O my God,
I put my hope in you
Because I am sure of your promises.
Deliver us, Lord, from every evil
And grant us peace in our day,
As we wait in joyful hope
For the coming of our Saviour, Jesus Christ.
~

Act of Love
O my God,
I love you with all my heart,
With all my soul, and with all my strength.
Lord, increase our love.
Help us to love one another.
~

Grace Before Meals
Bless us, O God, as we sit together.
Bless the food we eat today.
Bless the hands that made the food.
Bless us, O God. Amen.
~

Grace After Meals
Thank you, God, for the food we have eaten.
Thank you, God, for all our friends.
Thank you, God, for everything.
Thank you, God. Amen.
~

Prayer Before Communion
Lord Jesus, come to me.
Lord Jesus, give me your love.
Lord Jesus, come to me and give me yourself.
Lord Jesus, friend of children, come to me.
Lord Jesus, you are my Lord and my God.
Praise to you, Lord Jesus Christ.

Prayer After Communion
Lord Jesus, I love and adore you.
You're a special friend to me.
Welcome, Lord Jesus, O welcome.
Thank you for coming to me.

Thank you, Lord Jesus, O thank you
for giving yourself to me.
Make me strong to show your love
wherever I may be.

Be near me, Lord Jesus, I ask you to stay
close by me forever and love me, I pray.
Bless all of us children in your loving care
and bring us to heaven to live with you there.

I'm ready now, Lord Jesus,
to show how much I care.
I'm ready now to give your love
at home and everywhere. Amen.

Prayer For Forgiveness
O my God, help me to remember the times
when I didn't live as Jesus asked me to.
Help me to be sorry and to try again. Amen.
~
Prayer After Forgiveness
O my God, thank you for forgiving me.
Help me to love others.
Help me to live as Jesus asked me to. Amen.

Music Section

All of these songs are available on the accompanying CD

Advent Hymn
O Jesus, the source of all wisdom,
The one who will show the way of peace.
Be the light that burns so bright,
Lighting up our lives.

> *Prepare, prepare, prepare for the One who is coming.*
> *Prepare, prepare. Let us welcome him into our hearts.*

O Jesus, son of Mary,
Jesus, cousin of John;
Calling in the wilderness,
Calling for all to hear.

O Jesus, God is with us.
Emmanuel, the king of all kings;
Born in a manger, humble of birth,
Bringer of hope to the world.
~

All The Nations Of The Earth
> *All the nations of the earth praise the Lord*
> *Who brings to birth the greatest star, the smallest flower. Alleluia.*

Let the heavens praise the Lord. Alleluia.
Moon and stars praise the Lord. Alleluia.

Snow-capped mountains, praise the Lord. Alleluia.
Rolling hills, praise the Lord. Alleluia.

Deep sea water, praise the Lord. Alleluia.
Gentle rain, praise the Lord. Alleluia.

Roaring lion, praise the Lord. Alleluia.
Singing birds, praise the Lord. Alleluia.

Kings and princes, praise the Lord. Alleluia.
Young and old, praise the Lord. Alleluia.

Alleluia
Alleluia, Alleluia, Alleluia.
Alleluia, Alleluia, Alleluia.
Alleluia, Alleluia, Alleluia.
Alleluia, Alleluia, Alleluia.
~

Away In A Manger
Away in a manger, no crib for a bed,
The little Lord Jesus lay down his sweet head.
The stars in the bright sky looked down where he lay,
The little Lord Jesus asleep on the hay.

The cattle are lowing, the baby awakes,
But little Lord Jesus no crying he makes.
I love you Lord Jesus, look down from the sky
And stay by my bedside 'til morning is nigh.

Be near me Lord Jesus, I ask you to stay
Close by me forever and love me I pray.
Bless all the dear children in thy tender care
And fit us for heaven to live with you there.
~

Bless The Lord (Glory Be To The Father)
> *Bless the Lord, all that God has made.*
> *To God be glory and praise!*
> *Bless the Lord, all that God has made.*
> *To God be glory and praise!*

Glory be to the Father, and to the Son
And to the Holy Spirit;
As it was in the beginning
Is now and ever shall be,
World without end. Amen.

Christ Be Beside Me

Christ be beside me, Christ be before me,
Christ be behind me, King of my heart.
Christ be within me, Christ be below me,
Christ be above me, never to part.

Christ on my right hand, Christ on my left hand,
Christ all around me, shield in the strife.
Christ in my sleeping, Christ in my sitting,
Christ in my rising, light of my life.

Christ be in all hearts, thinking about me.
Christ be on all tongues, telling of me.
Christ be the vision, in eyes that see me,
In ears that hear me, Christ ever be.
~

Christ Be Our Light

Longing for light, we wait in darkness.
Longing for truth, we turn to you.
Make us your own, your holy people.
Light for the world to see.

Christ be our light! Shine in our hearts.
Shine through the darkness.
Christ be our light!
Shine in your Church gathered today.

Longing for food, many are hungry.
Longing for water, many still thirst.
Make us your bread, broken for others,
Shared until all are fed.

Longing for shelter, many are homeless.
Longing for warmth, many are cold.
Make us your building sheltering others,
Walls made of living stone.

Many the gifts, many the people,
Many the hearts that yearn to belong.
Let us be servants to one another,
Making your kingdom come.
~

Christ Is My Light

Christ is my light, lights up my days,
Fills me with joy, shows me the way,
Fills me with hope, fills me with peace,
Fills me with love that is gentle and free.

Circle Of Friends

You have friends, you are not alone.
Thanks to them, you're not on your own.
You are strong even when you feel small.
From the rain they will shelter you.
In your pain they will comfort you.
They will always pick you up when you fall.

Circle of friends all around you,
Circle of friends, strong and true,
Circle of friends always there for you.

Even when you are far apart,
To your friends you're joined heart to heart.
Far away you are not on your own.
You're not there but they think of you.
In their prayers they remember you.
You are never ever truly alone.
~

Close To You

I watch the sunrise lighting the sky,
Casting its shadows near.
And on this morning, bright though it be,
I feel those shadows near me.
But you are always close to me,
Following all my ways.
May I be always close to you,
Following all your ways, Lord.

I watch the sunlight shine through the clouds,
Warming the earth below.
And at the midday, life seems to say:
'I feel your brightness near me.'
For you are always close to me,
Following all my ways.
May I be always close to you,
Following all your ways, Lord.
~

Come And Be Born In Our Hearts

Come Lord Jesus, come Lord Jesus, come
Lord Jesus, come and be born in our hearts.

Come Emmanuel, come Emmanuel, come
Emmanuel, come and be born in our hearts.

Maranatha, Maranatha, Maranatha,
Come and be born in our hearts.

Come, O Prince of Peace, come O Prince of
Peace, come, O Prince of Peace, come and
be born in our hearts.

Our hearts are open, our hearts are open,
our hearts are open, come and be born in
our hearts.

~

Community Song
I am I, yes, I am me.
I'll be just who I'm made to be; I'm strong
And I can sing my own song.
There's no one I would rather be.
I'll live this life being true to me; I'm free.
I am happy to be me.

I am I, and we are we.
We share this special world.
We can be stronger now.
We are stronger when we know that we belong.
Different colours, different names,
Yet underneath we're all the same;
Community – that's what God wants us to be.

Refrain 1
All we have to say is let's all live this way,
Take time to care for people everywhere.
All we have to say is you can live this way,
So if you agree, come along and sing our song.

Refrain 2
The world's a wonder as it's spinning round in space.
We have to try and share, there is no other place.
No matter where you come from, this is still your home.
When you feel alone, don't be on your own.
You will find that friends are near.

We've all got a part you see,
A part in our community. We're strong,
When we help others to belong.
Help each other, share the fun;
There's a place for everyone.
So let's join in
With our community and sing.

Refrain 1

~

Eat This Bread
Eat this bread, drink this cup,
Come to me and never be hungry.
Eat this bread, drink this cup,
Trust in me and you will not thirst.

Anyone who eats this bread
Will live forever.

Go Now In Peace
Go now in peace together today.
Jesus is here in a very special way.
Tell all you meet that he is gentle and kind.
Praise him and love him in body, soul and mind.

Go in peace! Go in love!
Go in joy ev'ry girl and boy.
Go in peace! Go in love!
Go in joy ev'ry girl and boy.

Bring all the love we've had here today.
Share it around, don't let it fade away.
Love one another as Jesus Christ loves you.
Praise him and love him in everything you do.

~

Go Tell Everyone
God's Spirit is in my heart,
He has called me and set me apart.
This is what I have to do, what I have to do.

He sent me to give the good news to the poor,
Tell prisoners that they are prisoners no more,
Tell blind people that they can see
And set the downtrodden free.
And go tell everyone the news that the
kingdom of God has come, and go tell everyone
the news that God's kingdom has come.

Just as the Father sent me,
So I'm sending you out to be
My witnesses throughout the world,
The whole of the world.

Don't worry what you have to say,
Don't worry because on that day
God's Spirit will speak in your heart,
Will speak in your heart.

~

Happy In The Presence
Happy in the presence of the Lord.
We come and sing our praise to Lord Jesus,
Happy in the presence of the Lord.
We come and sing our praise to the Lord of all.

Come and share the bread of life,
bread that will feed us, help and protect us,
come and share the stories of old,
stories of Jesus, his work and his world.

Come and share the mem'ries we've had,
Happy days, sad days, days full of joy,

Music Section

Come to tell the Lord that we love
We'll live the life he told us to live.

~

Imagine You Were There

Imagine you were there on the Sunday.
Imagine you were there on that very day
Singing 'Hosanna! Blessed is he who comes in the Lord's name.'
Imagine you were there.

Imagine you were there on the Thursday
Gathering for prayer in the upper room.
'Do this in memory.
Love one another as I have loved you.'
Imagine you were there.

Imagine you were there on the Friday
With his mother Mary close to the cross,
Hearing him whisper:
'You will be with me this day in Paradise.'
Imagine you were there.

The sky turns dark.
He breathes his last.
He is gone.

Imagine you were there Easter morning,
Wondering where his body had gone.
Women rejoicing:
'Jesus is risen, raised to a new life!'
Imagine you were there.

~

Litany Of The Saints

Saint Gobnait, pray for us.
Deo gratias.*
Saint Gobnait, pray for us.
Deo gratias.*

Saint Patrick, pray for us.
Deo gratias.*
Saint Patrick, pray for us.
Deo gratias.*

Saint Brigid, pray for us.
Deo gratias.*
Saint Brigid, pray for us.
Deo gratias.*

Text omitted so that each school community may include its own patron saint.

All the saints, pray for us.
Deo gratias.*
All the saints, pray for us.
Deo gratias.*

*Deo gratias – Thanks be to God.

~

Magnificat

Hail! (2)
Hail Mary! (2)
Hail Mary, full of grace. (2)

My soul glorifies the Lord.
Hail Mary, full of grace.
My spirit rejoices in God my Saviour.
Hail Mary, full of grace.
He has done great things for me.
Hail Mary, full of grace.
Holy, holy, holy his name.
Holy, holy, holy his name.

Scattered the proud, filled the hungry.
Guarded the weak, not the mighty.
Showing his strength and his mercy.
Promised to Abraham long ago.
Holy, holy, holy his name.
Holy, holy, holy his name.

Repeat Chorus

~

Mary, Our Mother

Mary, our Mother, the Lord is with you.
Guide us, protect us, in all that we do.

We celebrate that on Easter Day
Jesus, Our Lord, is risen.

We celebrate on Ascension Day,
Jesus is taken to heaven.

We celebrate that on Pentecost Day,
God sends his Spirit to guide us.

We celebrate on Assumption Day,
Mary is taken to heaven.

Mary, our Mother, we crown you and say:
You are the Queen of Heaven.

Quiet And Still

I stretch my hands above my head I shake them all around,
I let them fall down slowly they won't make a sound,
I rest them on my knees I keep my body steady
My heart is beating quietly, I'm list'ning, now I'm ready.
I'm still, I'm still, I'm quiet and still,
I'm still, I'm quiet and still.

~

Remember Them

Remember, remember, remember those who've died,
With peace and rest may they be blessed,
May God be close beside,
May God be close beside.

God keep them, God bless them,
God shine your love on them,
Forever and forever, forever amen,
Forever more, amen.

Thank you, God, we love you.
Thank you, God, we pray.
Thank you, God, we love you.
Thank you day by day.

Repeat verse 1.

~

Song Of Repentance

We are watching in the dead of night.
We are waiting in the darkness still.
We are waiting for you, Lord, kind, forgiving Lord.
Come and bring your healing love.

We are longing for you, Lord, to come.
You are coming to forgive our sin.
We are longing for you, Lord, waiting for you, Lord,
Loving and forgiving Lord.

Like the sun that rises in the East,
You will light our world and give us love.
We are sure and certain, sure that you will come,
Come, O Lord, and listen to our prayer.

We are watching in the dead of night.
We are waiting in the darkness still.
We are waiting for you, Lord, kind and forgiving Lord,
Come and bring your healing love.
Waiting for you, Lord, kind, forgiving Lord,
Come and bring your healing love.

Spirit Anthem

Come, come, brighten this day,
Fire of the Spirit, fire of love.
Come, come, light up our way,
Fire of the Spirit, fire of love.

Holy Spirit, fill us anew.
Fire, wind and breath of God.
Holy Spirit, fill us anew.
Dancing now as we wait for you.

Come, come, move in our hearts,
Wind of the Spirit, live in me.
Come, come, move in our world,
Wind of the Spirit, blowing free.

Come, come, giver of life,
Breath of the Spirit, breath of God.
Come, come, giver of life,
Breathing within us, life and love.

~

Spirit-Filled Day

Oh what a Spirit-filled day this is,
What a Spirit-filled day, my Lord.
You have called us each by name,
We give ourselves to you on this Spirit-filled day.
What a Spirit-filled day, my Lord.
The Spirit gives us what we need
To live our lives each day.

The Spirit brings
Love – the Spirit lives!
Joy – the Spirit dances!
Peace – the Spirit rests!
Patience – the Spirit waits!
Kindness – the Spirit gives!
Goodness – the Spirit breathes!
Gentleness – the Spirit acts!
Faithfulness – the Spirit lasts!
Self-control – the Spirit cares!
The Spirit cares! The Spirit cares!

~

The Lord's Prayer (*Alive-O* Mass)

Our Father who art in heaven
Hallowed be thy name.
Thy kingdom come,
Thy will be done
On earth as it is in heaven.
Give us this day our daily bread.
Forgive us our trespasses
As we forgive those who trespass against us.
And lead us not into temptation
But deliver us from evil.

The Way To Be

Most of the time I'm good, I share,
My friends all like me, they know that I care.
Some of the time I'm mean, I fight,
But I know that when I'm like that it's not right.

Being selfish, being a bully,
That's not really me.
Being kind and being friendly,
That's the way to be!

Most of the time I'm fair, I'm true,
My friends all trust me, I'm glad that they do.
Some of the time I tell a lie,
Or leave someone out, and that makes them cry.

Being unfair and being untruthful,
That's not really me.
Being fair and being truthful,
That's the way to be!

~

They Care For Me

I have a family and I know that they care for me.
This is what they can do to show that they care for me.
They hold my hand but not too tight.
They care for me.

I have a family and I know that they care for me.
This is what they can do to show that they care for me.
They tuck me into bed at night, hold my hand but not too tight.
They care for me.

I have a family and I know that they care for me.
This is what they can do to show that they care for me.
They help me learn to read and write, tuck me into bed at night,
hold my hand but not too tight.
They care for me.

I have a family and I know that they care for me.
This is what they can do to show that they care for me.
They dry my tears after a fight, help me learn to read and write,
tuck me into bed at night, hold my hand but not too tight.
They care for me.

This Is The Day

Sing, sing, sing Alleluia,
This is the day the Lord has made.
Dance, dance, dance Alleluia,
This is the day the Lord has made.

Let us rejoice and be glad,
This is the day the Lord has made.
Let us rejoice and be glad,
This is the day.

Play music to honour his name.
This is the day the Lord has made.
Sing psalms and songs of praise.
This is the day.

~

Together Again

Together again, together again.
We're back! Together again.
With each new day we shout 'Hurray!'
It's good to be together again.

We're starting on a new adventure
Together ev'ry step of the way,
So much to learn, so much to say,
And God is with us as we pray.

There's me and you, there's teacher too,
We work together all the day through,
With songs to sing and games to play,
And God is with us as we pray.

~

Whatsoever You Do

Whatsoever you do to the least of my people,
That you do unto me.

When I was hungry you gave me to eat.
When I was thirsty you gave me to drink.
Now enter into the home of my Father.

When I was weary you helped me find rest.
When I was anxious you calmed all my fears.
Now enter into the home of my Father.

When I was aged you bothered to smile.
When I was restless you listened and cared.
Now enter into the home of my Father.

When I was laughed at you stood by my side.
When I was happy you shared in my joy.
Now enter into the home of my Father.

Within God's Creation

There's a world of showbiz all glamour and glitz.
There's a world of difference between my world and it.
There's a dream world in my head and right outside my door
There's a big wide wonderful world for me to explore.

Just as one voice can sing many different tunes,
Just as one house can have many different rooms,
Just as one head of hair has lots of different curls,
Within God's creation there are lots of different worlds.

There's a world of nature where things live and die.
There's an underwater world with strange fish that fly.
There's a world in every book and in my classroom too.
There's a world of work each day for me to get through.

There's a worldwide web where e-mails fly to and fro.
There's a world of information just so's you know.
I've an inner world, I sometimes go there when I pray,
But my favourite world of all is in our playground each day.
~

We Sing A Song To Brigid

We sing a song to Brigid,
Brigid brings the spring,
Awakens all the fields and the flowers
And calls the birds to sing.

All were welcome at her door
No-one was turned away
She loved the poor, the sick and the sore,
She helped them on their way.

She laid her cloak out on the ground
And watched it grow and grow
In wells and streams and fields of green
St Brigid's blessings flow.

Wilderness

Take time to turn away
To leave behind this busy world.
Take time out on our own
In a wilderness alone.

In the wilderness that's all around
Just turn and see what's to be found.
Close your eyes and see what you can see.
Think of all the friends you know
And let the love in your heart grow.
Be the very best that you can be.

In the wilderness you just might find
That when you turn and take the time,
You see things in a very different way.
Think of all the friends you know
And let the love in your heart grow.
Be the very best that you can be.

Dates of Feast Days

The following feast days are celebrated in *Prayer Assemblies for Primary Schools*:

- St Vincent de Paul – September 27
- Memorial of Guardian Angels – October 2
- St Francis of Assisi – October 4
- All Saints' Day – November 1
- All Souls' Day – November 2
- Advent always begins four Sundays before Christmas Day
- Immaculate Conception of Mary – December 8
- World Day of Peace – January 1
- Catholic Schools' Week is always celebrated during the last week in January
- St Brigid – February 1
- Feast of our Lady of Lourdes/World Day of the Sick – February 11
- St Valentine – February 14
- St Patrick – March 17
- St Joseph – March 19
- St Columba – June 9

The dates for the following feast days will change depending on when Easter Sunday is celebrated:

- Ash Wednesday is celebrated six weeks and four days before Easter Sunday
- Mother's Day
- The Solemnity of the Ascension is celebrated six weeks after Easter Sunday
- Pentecost Sunday is celebrated the week after the Solemnity of the Ascension, seven weeks after Easter Sunday
- The Solemnity of the Most Holy Trinity is celebrated on the Sunday after Pentecost Sunday, eight weeks after Easter Sunday
- The Feast of the Body and Blood of Christ (Corpus Christi) is celebrated on the Sunday after Trinity Sunday, nine weeks after Easter Sunday
- The Solemnity of the Most Sacred Heart of Jesus is celebrated nineteen days after Pentecost Sunday, which is also the Friday after Corpus Christi

The Perfect Accompaniment to your Prayer Assemblies!

Sacred Space Classroom Kit

Finally ... everything you need for your classroom sacred space in one box! Veritas are delighted to present the Sacred Space Classroom Kit. The aim of this kit is to provide resources for teachers and students to create a place for religious symbols in their classrooms: a sacred space. This space can be used as a focal point for prayer, and a means through which children will be enabled to express their own religious identity.

€45
£37
CODE: P91529

THE SACRED SPACE CLASSROOM KIT provides pictures, objects and different coloured cloths based on thirteen themes:

- Beginning the New School Year
- Mission awareness month (October)
- Remembering those who have died
- Advent and Christmas
- The Holy Family
- St Brigid and the Care of the Sick
- St Patrick's Day
- Lent
- Triduum
- Easter
- Mary (May)
- Pentecost
- Feast of the Body and Blood of Christ (Corpus Christi)

THREE WAYS TO SHOP:
In store | By phone | Online at www.veritas.ie

Abbey Street, Dublin 01 878 8177 | Blanchardstown Centre, Dublin 01 886 4030 | Cork 021 425 1255
Derry 028 7126 6888 | Ennis 065 682 8696 | Letterkenny 074 912 4814 | Monaghan 047 84077
Naas 045 856 882 | Sligo 071 916 1800 | DRC Bookshop, Belfast 028 9023 6249
Newry 028 3025 0321

VERITAS
www.veritas.ie